ATHLETE TO TRIATHLETE

Rockridge Press publishes its books in a variety of electronic and print formats. Some content that appears in print may not be available in electronic books, and vice versa.

TRADEMARKS: Rockridge Press and the Rockridge Press logo are trademarks or registered trademarks of Callisto Media Inc. and/or its affiliates, in the United States and other countries, and may not be used without written permission. All other trademarks are the property of their respective owners. Rockridge Press is not associated with any product or vendor mentioned in this book.

Interior and Cover Designer: Michael Cook
Art Producer: Sue Bischofberger
Editor: Rachel Feldman
Production Manager: Martin Worthington
Production Editor: Melissa Edeburn

Cover illustration: © draco77vector/shutterstock and © Ville heikkinen/shutterstock.

Interior illustration: © Christian Papazoglakis/Illozoo.

Photography: © Pavel1964/iStock, p. x; © pixdeluxe/iStock, p. x; © vm/iStock, pp. x and 38; © nadianb/shutterstock, p. 10; © etorres/shutterstock, p. 26; © ArtistGNDphotography/iStock, p, 48; © oneinchpunch/shutterstock, p. 58; © HKPNC/iStock, p. 68; © Nutthaseth Van/shutterstock, p. 76; © Ivanko80/shutterstock, p. 100; © FatCamera/iStock, p. 118; © sirtravelalot/shutterstock, p. 174.

Author photo courtesy of Joey Mock.

ISBN: Print 978-1-64152-552-7
Ebook 978-1-64152-553-4

R0

*To every cyclist, runner, swimmer, and fitness enthusiast
who made the courageous decision to become a three-sport athlete.*

ATHLETE TO TRIATHLETE

The Ultimate Triathlon Training Plan for
Sprint and Olympic Races

Marni Sumbal, MS, RD, CSSD, LD/N

ROCKRIDGE
PRESS

CONTENTS

MEET YOUR COACH //

Maybe you swam in college and miss the camaraderie of being part of a squad. Per-haps past running injuries have made you tri-curious. Or maybe you are seeking a new challenge as a devoted cyclist. Regardless of your fitness background, triathlon is an everybody sport. Triathletes are encouraging, disciplined, motivating, and sup-portive. No wonder so many people are taking the leap and giving triathlon a try. Just watch any triathlon event, and you will undoubtedly feel inspired.

For the past 13 years, I've called myself a triathlete. I've participated in all types of triathlon events from sprint to long distance, aquabike to aquathlon. My favorite is the Ironman, and I've successfully completed 16 of these 140.6-mile events. Prior to embarking on this incredibly fun multisport lifestyle, I participated in running events. Before that, I dedicated more than 10 years of my life to competitive swimming. Near the end of my college education, I heard about a local triathlon event. I welcomed it as a challenging new training adventure and a way to meet other people. I feel so for-tunate that I discovered triathlon—it has allowed me to travel to new places, develop long-lasting friendships, and discover my unique talents and strengths.

My formal education is in sport nutrition and exercise physiology. Although I've applied my understanding of exercise, nutrition, and training to my own triathlon journey, nothing compares to the reward of being a triathlon coach and helping so many athletes achieve personal successes and cross a once-unthinkable finish line. Triathlon can teach you many valuable life lessons, like perseverance, confidence, optimism, commitment, and time management.

Although triathlon has evolved since I first entered the sport, one thing has remained the same: Through hard work, patience, and determination, you can accomplish feats that you never thought were possible by your body and mind.

See you at the finish line.

ONE

TRIATHLON 101

Triathlon is a relatively modern sport. Originating in France in the 1920s, a 3-kilometer (km) run, a 12-km bike, and a swim across the Marne River made up the first "Les Trois Sports." Five decades later, triathlon had its birth in the United States. Organized by Don Shanahan and Jack Johnstone of the San Diego Track Club, the first triathlon event took place on September 25, 1974. Forty-six athletes, mostly from local running clubs, participated in the 10km (6.2-mile) run, 8km (4.9-mile) bike, and 500m (.31-mile) swim. In 1978, the Ironman triathlon was founded. With only 15 courageous athletes at the start line, the Hawaii Ironman triathlon—originated by John and Judy Collins—helped settle a debate as to who was the fittest athlete. Combining three iconic races—The Waikiki Roughwater Swim, the Around Oahu Bike Race, and the Honolulu Marathon—the winner would be titled "The Ironman." Today, this 140.6-mile (226km) event with a 17-hour time limit continues to receive widespread media coverage and attention. Since 1981, Kona, Hawaii, has remained the home of the annual Ironman World Championship and continues to be viewed as the most honored and prestigious triathlon event in the world.

In 2000, triathlon became an Olympic sport at the Summer Games in Sydney, Australia. The official Olympic-distance triathlon features a 1500m (.93-mile) swim, a 40km (24.8-mile) bike, and a 10km (6.2-mile) run. In 2014, the National Collegiate Athletic Association (NCAA) approved women's triathlon as an emerging sport. In 2017, more than 360,000 people in the United States took part in a triathlon event, with the sprint triathlon ranking as the most popular. With the combined help of USA Triathlon, The International Triathlon Union (ITU), the World Triathlon Corporation (WTC), Challenge Family, and many grassroots multisport organizations, participation in the sport of triathlon continues to grow all over the world.

WHY TRI

Training for a triathlon adds purpose to your everyday exercise regime. From improving health to boosting self-confidence, overcoming fear, stretching physical limits, or becoming a role model, the attractions of being a three-sport athlete are inescapable.

That said, it's normal to feel a bit overwhelmed by the challenges of this multi-sport endeavor. Intimidated by all the gear used in a triathlon? Although triathlon is an equipment-heavy sport compared with running, it doesn't have to break the bank. Uncertain about balancing training for three sports with work, family, and life? By having realistic expectations about the time you can dedicate to training, you can build your training around your life and still achieve your fitness goals.

Because it's easy to be overenthusiastic when starting a new hobby, I caution you not to compromise important parts of your life (e.g., nutrition and sleep) to fit in more training than you can handle. I never want you to sacrifice your health for performance. Even if you come from a strong fitness background, it's important to find the best training prescription for you, within the framework of your life. My best advice is to start conservatively and remain flexible. Above all, optimize your available training hours by focusing on quality over quantity. This strategy will ensure a fun, enriching, and sustainable triathlon journey.

CHOOSING AND ENTERING A RACE

When you're just starting out, I suggest getting your feet wet with a short-distance triathlon. As you gain endurance, resiliency, and racing experience, you'll be better prepared to handle the demands of long-course racing. Regardless of the race distance, you don't have to complete the exact distances in training that you will be completing on race day. Triathlon training is a unique sport in that there are many creative ways to improve race readiness. Through two-a-day workouts, strength training, relatively long training sessions on the weekends, and brick sessions (egaging in sport disciplines one after the other, with little break between), you can gain the cardiovascular fitness, muscular strength, and mental stamina needed to feel prepared for race day.

As for the sport itself, triathlon has grown in participation since its inception, but the standard distances remain the same.

EVENT	SWIM	BIKE	RUN	REGISTRATION FEE
SPRINT	0.5 miles (750m)	12.4 miles (20km)	3.1 miles (5km)	~$85-120
OLYMPIC	0.93 miles (1.5km)	24.8 miles (40km)	6.2 miles (10km)	~$130-175
HALF (70.3 miles)	1.2 miles (1.9km)	56 miles (90km)	13.1 miles (21.09km)	~$225-350
FULL (140.6 miles)	2.4 miles (3.8km)	112 miles (180km)	26.2 miles (42.2km)	~$700-850

When training for your first triathlon, I suggest dedicating at least twelve weeks to prepare for the event. Rushing the process often leads to injury or burnout. A half or full-distance triathlon may sound epic, but a short-distance race can give you the challenge you're seeking without the risk of taking on too much too quickly.

When selecting your first triathlon event, consider these factors:

Pool vs. open water swim: If you lack a swimming background, a triathlon with a pool swim is a perfect way to start your triathlon career.

Typical race-day weather conditions: Although you can't control the weather, you can plan for it. An early-season race (February–April) will require winter training and you may have cool temps on race day. A late season race (May–August) will give you more time to train in warm conditions but you may experience brutally hot (or rainy) race-day conditions. What weather suits you best for training and racing?

Course logistics and terrain: With so many firsts to be experienced on race day, it's good to limit stressful situations. An event with plenty of on-site parking, one transition area, a wave start, adequate volunteers, an easy-to-navigate course, and a venue close to home is likely to give you a low-stress first-time experience. Depending on your fitness background, consider a course that suits your athletic strengths.

Race reputation: Triathlon events are known to provide helpful volunteers, friendly race staff, and a fun, supportive atmosphere, but you might want to select a race that has a great reputation as a beginner-friendly event.

When searching for a race, websites like Active.com and Trifind.com cover all triathlon events, making it easy to select races. You can narrow down your search by selecting race specifics like beginner, women only, kids, off-road, or short distance. Races can also be categorized by location and month.

When you register for an event, it's important to select the right category. By putting yourself into a specific division, you are more likely to race—and be ranked—among athletes of a similar ability. Depending on the race, awards are given to the overall male and female finishers as well as to the top few male and female athletes in each division.

Race categories may include (but are not limited to):

- Open (elite)
- Age group (e.g., 40–44M, 30–34F)
- Novice
- Masters (40+ years of age)
- Clydesdale/Athena (based on weight minimums, 220 pounds and 165 pounds respectively)
- Paratriathlon (athletes with a physical impairment)
- Relay (a two- or three-person team)

Most races provide registration fees based on a fixed price-increase schedule. Registering several months (rather than a few weeks) before the event will save you money. Most races close online registration on race week, but may offer on-site, race-day registration. Your race entry fee goes toward swag (e.g., T-shirt or hat), finisher medal, race photos (typically at an additional cost), post-race food, awards, timed results, and a memorable race experience. If you are not a USA Triathlon (USAT) annual member, you will need to pay a one-day membership with your registration for a USAT-sanctioned event. Annual members are required to bring their membership card to registration at a USAT-sanctioned event. Most races do not offer refunds, transfers, or exchanges of registrations.

MENTAL FITNESS

Your thoughts impact your everyday actions, which means they can be empowering or destructive. For example, a bad mood can leave you unmotivated to train and doubtful of your physical abilities. You must learn to control what you think.

Acquiring mental fortitude doesn't happen overnight. Like any skill, it's developed through experience and practice. If you want your body to perform a certain way, capitalizing on your mental fitness will ensure that you can fully express your physical capabilities on race day. One of the biggest challenges of mental training is that the benefits are not tangible. You can improve your running pace, but you can't measure confidence.

The Three Cs

A strong and healthy mind-set allows you to rise to the challenges and opportunities that life presents to you. Keep these three Cs in mind:

Commitment means that you are dedicated to your training. With clear goals, a process-driven mind-set, and a positive outlook, you'll sustain the motivation needed to keep you going. Commitment doesn't mean that you are so focused on your athletic goals that everything else in your life becomes unimportant. Within the scope of your limitations—work, family, travel—triathlon training and racing should be an enjoyable commitment that you want to make time for on a daily basis.

Confidence plays a key role in your performance. Some days you'll feel great about yourself and other days you'll be your own worst enemy. To perform to your abilities, you must first believe in yourself. Whenever you doubt your abilities, remind yourself that you are good enough and capable enough. Most of all, shut down negative self-talk and never compare yourself to others (or a past version of yourself).

Care means making time for yourself without going to the extreme. Most athletes take great pride in being mentally and physically tough, but far too many athletes associate their self-worth with their fitness, body image, or performance. To keep a sense of balance, remember that triathlon isn't your life—it's part of your lifestyle.

Don't sacrifice time with friends and family for more training. Don't destroy your health through dieting to achieve an idealized body composition. Make time for rest, relaxation, cooking, sleep, and self-care. At the same time, it's not selfish to dedicate a bit of time each day to your hobby. Keeping your perspective on how triathlon fits in your life will help you get the most out of training without compromising your physical and mental health.

Staying Motivated

When motivation is high, it's easy to envision yourself crossing the finish line with a victorious fist pump. It's the follow-through, action part of training that can be difficult to sustain. That's why motivation is important. When you are tired, busy, or dealing with a setback, you need purpose and direction to drive your actions. Every human being has a different source of motivation. For some, it's a goal or incentive, like reaching a personal best time. Others may be motivated by health, a personal cause, or mental well-being.

If you find yourself struggling with motivation, you are never alone. Even professional athletes, who train for a living, often struggle to find the drive to train.

Use these practical strategies when you find yourself in a mental rut:

Know your "why." At times, training may feel repetitive and boring. If a personal challenge is greater than your why, triathlon will feel like an unnecessary sacrifice. When you know exactly what you want to achieve and why, it's a lot easier to put in the work, even when you don't feel like it.

It's okay to fail. When something doesn't go as planned, it's easy to give up. When you experience a setback, learn from it. Mistakes and failures provide you with valuable feedback—lessons you can use to improve.

Change your training conditions. Freshen up your music playlist, explore a new environment, or invite a friend to come along. Because repetition can become mind numbing, give yourself a mental boost by revitalizing your workout regime.

Train for those who can't. If you are struggling with motivation, tap into something that really matters to you. Think of someone who is going through a difficult time or a cause that you are passionate about. There's great power in dedicating a workout to someone or something.

Re-energize yourself in a group setting. You are more motivated to train when others hold you accountable, but nothing is better than the camaraderie of physical suffering.

Don't be all or nothing. Routines and plans are helpful, but not if they are overly rigid. Being a self-proclaimed perfectionist can cause frustration and burnout. Put your energy into what you can control, recognizing that something is better than nothing. Manage your expectations and focus on progress, not perfection.

5 Tips for Staying Calm on Race Day

1. Welcome your race-day jitters. Butterflies are a necessary part of the racing process. They are your body's way of telling you that you are prepared and ready. As soon as the gun goes off, the adrenaline will wash away pre-race anxiety.

2. Anxiety causes rapid and shallow breathing, which may result in an increase in heart rate, dizziness, and tension. When you feel nervous, focus on slow, deep breathing from your belly.

3. Stay in the now. Let the outcome take care of itself. Process-oriented execution and living in the moment help you focus on what you need to do to deliver the best outcome possible.

4. Focus on what you can control. Directing energy to anyone or anything other than yourself can make you feel tense, nervous, or doubtful.

5. Have fun! If you put too much pressure on yourself or become too serious, you'll take the enjoyment out of racing. Race day is a celebration of your hard work!

Handling Pressure

As an athlete, pressure will always be part of your life. Triathlon may be challenging, but it shouldn't be a high-pressure sport. Pressure is the perception of a threat, which means it's often nothing more than a product of your imagination. The thought of failing, not reaching a desired outcome, underperforming, making mistakes, or disappointing others can manifest as increased heart rate, rapid breathing, self-doubt, fear, and anxiety. When you "feel" pressure, it's likely that you are worried about an outcome or what others will think of you. As a result, you may underperform or sabotage your performance with silly mistakes.

Because it's easy to get in your own way, use mantras to help you return to a state of calm:

- I am doing this for me.
- Yes, I can.
- Be in the now.
- I trained for this experience.
- Success will find me today.
- I am capable.
- Be present.
- Don't be afraid to fail.
- I control how I feel.
- Forward progress.
- Just keep moving.
- Thank you, body.
- Today is my day.
- My best is good enough.

The more experience you gain from training and racing, the more confidence you'll have in your abilities. Above all, the outcome of one workout or race is not a litmus test of your self-worth. Don't forget that triathlon should be a fun and joyful hobby that contributes to a fulfilling and meaningful life.

TWO

NUTRITION

///////////////////////////////////////→

Every day it seems like new ground-breaking sports nutrition research surfaces—and with good reason. Nutrition plays an important role in exercise physiology, performance, health, and recovery. Every athlete has unique nutritional requirements dependent on their training program, body composition goals, genetics, and fitness level, so there is no one best diet to follow. Moreover, your nutritional requirements, food choices, and strategies will change throughout the year, depending on training volume and intensity.

Even during peak training, when energy requirements are increased, your food choices should always be nutritious and health promoting. Leaving your diet to chance may result in nutrient-poor food choices. But a diet of restriction, rigidity, and obsession will lead to less-than-optimal energy availability to support your active lifestyle. Food prep, food variety, and nutrient timing will help optimize your training diet, especially when you feel like life is one uninterrupted series of training, eating, working, and sleeping.

YOUR TRAINING DIET

Being well-nourished puts your body into a state of optimal functioning. Your body's primary fuel sources during exercise include stored fat (in the form of triglycerides in adipose, or fat, tissue) and glycogen (digested carbohydrates stored in the muscles, liver, and bloodstream). Depending on workout intensity or duration, your body will select the most efficient fuel sources for the job, and the quantity of each to use for energy production. Body fat stores are in abundant supply in every body type, whereas carbohydrates are in short supply due to limited stores in the muscles and liver. Although muscle protein can provide energy, breaking down your muscle tissue is not ideal because it stresses the immune system. To prevent this situation, consume adequate carbohydrates and calories on a daily basis.

Unless you suffer from a food allergy or intolerance, or need to avoid certain foods for ethical, religious, or health reasons, your diet should not include an "off-limit" food list. The key to building a healthy sports diet is to consume a variety of nutrient-dense foods from all food groups. A well-balanced diet should include

Carbohydrates: Your body's main source of energy to fuel your brain, muscles, and central nervous system. Great sources include potatoes, rice, whole grains, fruits, vegetables, dairy, and legumes.

Protein: Needed to support the growth, repair, and maintenance of muscles, tissues, tendons, ligaments, nails, hair, and skin. Prioritize real-food sources, rich in amino acids, over heavily processed protein bars. Great sources include eggs, chicken, fish, red meat, dairy, tofu, tempeh, edamame, beans, and lentils.

Fats: Needed to transport and absorb fat-soluble vitamins (A, D, E, and K), support cell growth, protect organs, provide energy to the body, and make meals satisfying (and flavorful). Great sources include olive oil, avocado, butter, cheese, nuts, seeds, nut butter, and fish.

Vitamins and minerals: Essential for metabolism, building tissue, maintaining fluid balance, carrying oxygen, supporting bone health, and reducing oxidative stress. Focus on foods rich in calcium, iron, zinc, magnesium, potassium, vitamin D, B vitamins, and antioxidants.

Water: Water is the main component of your body. It protects your brain and spinal cord, lubricates joints, aids in digestion, eliminates waste products, plays a role in body temperature regulation, and is the primary component of sweat. Fluid recommendations are 90 to 120 ounces/per day (for women and men, respectively).

One of the biggest nutritional challenges for athletes is figuring out how much energy from food is needed to support training. Your daily caloric intake is made up of the three macronutrients: carbohydrates, protein, and fat. Use this chart to help determine your daily macronutrient needs based on your weight, activity duration, and intensity.

Daily Macronutrient Needs

DAILY ACTIVITY	CARB INTAKE	PROTEIN INTAKE	FAT INTAKE
30–60 minutes; low intensity/very light activity	3–5 grams per kilogram of body weight per day	1.4–1.6g/kg	1g/kg
60–90 minutes; low to moderate activity	4–6g/kg/d	1.5–1.6g/kg	1g/kg
45–75 minutes; moderate to high intensity	5–7g/kg/d	1.6–1.8g/kg	1g/kg
90 minutes–3 hours; moderate to high intensity	6–8g/kg/d	1.8g/kg	1g/kg
3+ hours; low to moderate intensity	8–10g/kg/d	1.8g/kg	1g/kg

1 lb = 2.2 kg

For example, Jane weighs 150 lbs (68kg) and is training 60 to 90 minutes a day. Her daily energy needs will look like this:

Carbohydrate: 68kg x 4–6g = 272–408g (1088–1632 calories*)

Protein: 68kg x 1.5–1.6g = 102–109g (408–436 calories*)

Fat: 68kg x 1g = 68g (612 calories*)

Total calories/day: 2108–2680 (high calorie range on higher volume/intensity days)

*Carbs: 4 calories per gram

*Protein: 4 calories per gram

*Fat: 9 calories per gram

What you eat between workouts will affect how well you perform and recover from one training session to the next. High-intensity and high-volume training sessions deplete muscle and liver glycogen stores much faster than low-intensity, low-volume training sessions. They are also more taxing on your bones, muscles, heart, and immune system. Accordingly, your carbohydrate intake varies on a day-to-day basis. In other words, your carb intake is based on your workout load. With little variation to your daily fat intake, your protein needs will slightly increase on high-intensity or high-volume training days due to the stress placed on your muscles and bones. Varying the quantity of each macro (instead of obsessing over calories) will help you boost fitness, recover faster, protect your immune system and bone health, optimize body composition, and, most of all, help you get more out of your active lifestyle.

Eating Around Workouts

Eating the right foods, timed appropriately with your workout, can help you get more out of your training sessions.

Before Workouts

Eating the right pre-workout snack (or meal) will

- Top off muscle glycogen stores
- Delay glycogen depletion
- Provide immediate fuel and fluid during the early part of exercise
- Prevent hunger pains
- Refill liver glycogen stores (especially after an overnight fast) to reduce the risk of hypoglycemia
- Optimize fluid levels to minimize dehydration
- Provide a psychological edge

Most triathletes will eat 30 to 60 minutes prior to exercise. Consider energy-dense carbohydrates (packing a lot of carbs per bite) that are low in fat and fiber. White bread, applesauce, bananas, oatmeal, rice, or potatoes are easy to digest and leave minimal residue in the gut. Although most of your pre-workout calories should come from carbohydrates, adding a small amount of protein and fat will help slow down digestion, especially if you are a carb-sensitive athlete who experiences hypoglycemic symptoms (e.g., lightheadedness or dizziness) before or during the first 20 minutes in a workout. Select foods that can be replicated on race day—foods that are easy to find, easy to prepare, and easy to consume. A good example would be a slice of white toast (or an English muffin) with a spoonful of nut butter and a generous drizzle of honey. As a general guideline, allow:

- 3 to 4 hours to digest a large meal (450–600 calories)
- 1.5 to 3 hours for a medium-sized meal (250–450 calories)
- 0.5 to 1.5 hours for a mini meal or snack (100–250 calories)

During Workouts

You may be able to complete training sessions with only water, but a triathlon requires a well-practiced fueling plan to minimize dehydration and glycogen depletion. If you consume only water during your longer or more intense training sessions, your muscle glycogen and blood glucose stores may drop to low levels, your risk of dehydration will increase (and hyponatremia, a low level of sodium in the blood, may result), your recovery will be compromised, and your immune system may be threatened.

Although your daily training diet will help you adapt to training stress, it's important to consume well-formulated sport nutrition products during certain workouts. Unlike real food, sport drinks, gels, and energy blocks or chews are marketed to triathletes because they are portable, convenient, and easy to consume during swimming, biking, and running. These engineered products provide a specifically formulated amount of fluids, carbohydrates, and sodium that can be easily digested and absorbed during exercise. Sports bars and real food sources like bananas or homemade rice balls are typically reserved for long-duration, lower-intensity training sessions.

Because most triathletes complain of GI (gastrointestinal) issues as a primary limiter on race day, it's important to train your gut to tolerate taking in calories and fluids while exercising. By regularly consuming sport nutrition products during your workouts, you'll increase the odds of avoiding unpleasant symptoms such as cramping, bloating, dizziness, nausea, extreme fatigue, and a sloshing stomach.

Recommended Carb Intake per Hour During Exercise

TYPE OF ACTIVITY	RECOMMENDED CARB AND ELECTROLYTE INTAKE PER HOUR	CONSIDERATIONS
Less than 45 minutes, low intensity	Carbohydrate and electrolytes are not required.	Water is recommended. Added sodium (electrolyte beverage) will decrease extreme sweat loss. A hint of sugar may provide a psychological boost.
High-intensity exercise lasting 45–75 minutes	30–50g carbohydrate 250–400mg sodium 20–24 fluid ounces	Choose glucose, fructose, or maltodextrin as the primary ingredient. Drink on a schedule—take 2–4 gulps every 10–15 minutes.
Endurance and high-intensity exercise lasting 1–3 hours and on race day.	Per hour: 30–60g carbohydrate 250–1000mg sodium 24–32 fluid ounces	Prioritize liquid calories from a sport drink containing multiple sources of carbohydrates (ex. glucose, fructose, or maltodextrin). Opt for mild-tasting flavors. After ~90 minutes, it's okay to nibble on solid food (~50 calories every 20–30 minutes) to keep the tummy happy. Food and/or liquid sources should be palatable and slightly (but not overly) sweet. A variety of flavors for both fluid and food is encouraged to prevent taste bud fatigue. Drink on a schedule: 3–5 gulps every 10–15 minutes.

After Workouts

Recovery is a continuous process—one that occurs from one training session to the next. The more organized you are with your meals and snacks, the quicker your recovery will be. The better you fuel and hydrate before and during the workout, the more effective your recovery process will be. Rehydration with water and sodium are top priorities after intense or high-volume training sessions. Additionally, the post-workout consumption of carbohydrates and protein may help restore muscle glycogen, repair damaged muscle tissue, and provide important nutrients for your immune system.

It's not uncommon for triathletes to lack the drive to eat and to crave only water after an intense, long, or hot workout. Therefore, after a workout, thirst and appetite are not reliable methods of determining how much fluid, sodium, and calories are needed to adequately recover. Whether you consume a snack or a meal depends on the type of training session completed, the timing of your next workout, and what is convenient for you.

Consume a post-workout snack within 30 minutes of exercising if:

- Your workout is of high intensity or long volume
- Muscle damage has occurred (e.g., through plyometrics or weight-bearing activity)
- Your workout included eccentric movements (e.g., downhill running or strength training)
- There are fewer than eight hours until your next workout
- You can't eat a meal within 30 minutes of your workout

A good example of a post-workout snack would be 8 ounces of milk or milk alternative (with 8-plus grams of protein), a banana, a handful of granola, and a glass of water. Then, when you are ready, consume a balanced meal.

Skip the engineered foods and shakes and consume a healthy, well-balanced meal within 20 to 30 minutes of exercising if:

- You only exercise once a day and have long recovery periods between two workouts
- Your workout is neither intense nor high in volume (e.g., low to moderate intensity for no more than 75 minutes)
- You are hungry for a meal soon after a workout

A good example of a post-workout meal would be two slices of bread (or 1/2 cup dry oats plus toppings) with 1 tablespoon each of butter and jam, a handful of spinach with 2 eggs, mixed veggies, 1/2 avocado, olive oil, and salt, along with 16–24 ounces of fluid.

Determining Your Hydration Needs

Because sweat rates and fluid intake change throughout the season and vary by athlete, it's impossible to enforce a one-size-fits-all fluid and electrolyte replacement schedule. Some athletes may tolerate a 2 or 3 percent loss of body weight with no effect on performance. On the other hand, athletes who exercise in hot and humid environments, especially at high intensity or a long time, need to be extra cautious. A hydration strategy must be based on workout intensity, duration, and environmental conditions. The goal is to prevent more than a 2 percent drop in body weight from fluid loss.

One way to determine your needs is to calculate your sweat rate. Your pre-exercise weight minus your post-exercise weight (in pounds), plus fluid intake (in ounces) during the activity, equals your individual hourly sweat rate. Every 1 pound lost is equal to 16 ounces of fluid. Weigh yourself in the nude. Urination or a bowel movement during the workout will throw off the calculation.

EXAMPLE

Pre-workout weight: 140 lbs.
Post-workout weight: 139 lbs.
Volume of water consumed during 1-hour workout: 12 oz.
Fluid deficiency (pre-workout weight minus post-workout weight): 140 – 139 = 1 lb. (or 16 oz.)
Total sweat loss: 16 oz. + 12 oz. = 28 oz. per hour
Sweat rate: 28 oz. per hour

Recovery Days

When it comes to active rest and recovery—two critical components of your training plan—it's common for athletes to dramatically cut out calories or avoid carbohydrates when energy expenditure is low. Or, they might view a rest day as a "cheat" day and consume too much of a food they normally avoid.

Much of your daily nutrition centers around calories and carbohydrates, both of which are important fuel sources for the brain and muscles. For example, on days with lower energy expenditure (e.g., lighter training days or days off), there should only be a slight adjustment in your caloric intake (primarily from carbohydrates). Given that a day off from training (or an active recovery day) is intended to help you recover from previous training stress, dramatically restricting calories, skipping meals or snacks, and avoiding carbohydrates entirely may undermine your immune system, cause restless sleep, and result in a performance setback. Because going long hours without eating may result in evening overeating, uncomfortable hunger, a decline in blood sugar, moodiness, low energy, and sweet cravings, aim to eat every 2 to 3 hours and prioritize wholesome foods—which nature intended you to eat.

	CARBOHYDRATE INTAKE	PROTEIN INTAKE	FAT INTAKE
HOW MUCH	3–5 grams per kilogram of body weight	1.5–1.6g/kg	1g/kg
TIPS	50–80g per meal 30–40g per snack	20–30g per meal 5–10g per snack	~10–20g fat at each meal ~5–10g per snack

Body Image

Within the sport of triathlon, it's not uncommon for athletes to manipulate their diet to lower body fat percentage. Whether for aesthetics, competitive leanness, body dissatisfaction, or pursuit of an ideal "race weight," an innocent attempt to lose a few pounds can easily spiral out of control, undermining health, training, recovery, performance, and mental well-being. Although there are safe and healthy ways to change body composition, it's not uncommon for athletes to engage in unhealthy weight-loss methods, such as dieting, avoiding food groups, and over-exercising, resulting in negative emotional and physical consequences.

Preparing for a triathlon should never require obsessive training and restrictive eating. As you build your fitness, build a better body image. In today's fad-diet obsessed society, it can be difficult to keep a healthy perspective on how your body looks in the mirror. I'm here to tell you that you can be a triathlete at any weight. Triathletes come in all shapes and sizes. Every triathlete has his or her own optimum performance weight—the weight where the body functions the best—and this body type is achieved by consistent training, nutritious eating, and proper fueling and hydration (and genetics). If you are concerned about body image, remember that a performance-ready body is more about how you feel and perform than what the scale or the mirror tells you.

Your training and diet should promote long-term health and longevity in sport. Eating is not cheating. If you need personalized nutrition assistance, reach out to a board-certified sport dietitian for help.

RACE-DAY NUTRITION

A haphazard race-day fueling plan may jeopardize all the hard work you put into training. Although your race-day nutrition plan will evolve with experience, having a plan as to what and when you will consume on race day will help you perform at your best while reducing the risk of GI distress, dehydration, and early fatigue.

Sprint

Although the race may be short, your goal is to be nutritionally prepared going into the event. Stick with easily tolerated foods (low in fat/fiber) and stay sufficiently hydrated in the 48 hours before the race. Other than that, no major dietary changes are needed.

WHEN	HOW MUCH	TIPS
Pre-Race: ~2.5–3 hours before start	~0.8–1g carbohydrate per pound of body weight ~10–15g protein/fat 16–20 ounces water ~1/4 teaspoon table salt (~575 mg sodium)	Choose well-tolerated foods, low in fat/fiber.
Pre-Race: ~90 minutes before start	12–16 ounces sport drink (~90–120 calories)	No more solid food. Trust that your muscles are stocked with fuel.
Pre-Race: ~20 min before race start	8–12 ounces water	Optional: Take a gel/energy chew (~80–100 calories) and wash down with water. Avoid caffeinated gels unless well-tolerated.

WHEN	HOW MUCH	TIPS
Swim	Nothing	Wait until you are 10-15 minutes on the bike to begin taking in fluids/calories.
Bike	1 sport drink bottle containing: ~24–28 ounce water ~40–50g carbohydrates (~160-200 calories) ~400–800mg sodium Take 4–5 chugs every 10–15 minutes.	Since the GI system is relatively stable on the bike, this is the most opportune time to take in fuel, fluids, and electrolytes. Frequent consumption, in small amounts, will optimize digestion— especially if it's hot outside. Practice with your race-day fueling plan in training to be fully prepared.
Run	Option 1: Consume 2–3 sips of a sport drink at each aid station (~every 8–12 minutes). Option 2: Wear a hydration belt/pack and plan to consume 10 ounces of fluid, 80–100 calories and 250–400mg sodium (in the form of a sport drink) every 30 minutes of running. Take 1–2 sips every 8–10 minutes. Use aid stations for sipping/cooling with water. Option 3: Consume a swig of a gel before each aid station and wash down with water. Plan to finish one gel every 30–45 minutes of running.	For easy consumption and better absorption of a gel, dilute your gel by squeezing it into a small handheld flask and top with water. Do this before the race start so your gel flask is ready for the run. Fueling and hydrating on the run can be challenging. It may not be comfortable and it's not always convenient to bring fluids with you. Although the race course will provide fluids at aid stations, you need to train your stomach (in training sessions) to take in fluid and fuel while running. This may take up to 6 weeks to train your gut.

Olympic

Although elite athletes will complete this distance in less than 2.5 hours, the majority of triathletes will require 3–3 ½ hours to complete an Olympic distance event. Whereas you can get away with under-fueling in a sprint, it's critical to practice and perfect your race-day fueling/hydration plan in training for an Olympic distance event. This semi-long duration triathlon requires a careful balance of proper pacing and adequate fluid/fuel consumption. Stick with easily tolerated foods (low in fat/fiber) and stay sufficiently hydrated in the 48 hours going into the race. Due to tapering, it's not necessary to overhaul your diet to be primarily carbohydrate-based. Continue to eat a nourishing diet—low in fat and fiber—but emphasize carbohydrates in the morning in the two days before the race to top off muscle and liver glycogen stores.

WHEN	HOW MUCH	TIPS
Pre-Race: ~2.5–3 hours before start	~1–2 grams carbohydrates per pound of body weight ~10–15g protein/fat 16–20 ounces water ~500–800mg sodium (~1/4–1/3 teaspoon salt)	Choose well-tolerated foods, low in fat/fiber.
Pre-Race: ~90 minutes before start	12–16 ounces sport drink (~90–120 calories)	No more solid food. Trust that your muscles are stocked with fuel.
Pre-Race: ~20 min before start	8–12 ounces water	Optional: Take a gel/energy chew (~80–100 calories) and wash down with water.

WHEN	HOW MUCH	TIPS
Swim	Nothing	Wait until you are 10-15 minutes on the bike to begin taking in fluids/calories.
Bike	2x sport drink bottles, each containing: ~24–28 ounce water ~50–60g carbohydrates (~200-240 calories) ~400–800mg sodium Take 4–5 chugs every 10–15 minutes.	Since the GI system is relatively stable on the bike, this is the most opportune time to take in fuel, fluids, and electrolytes. Frequent consumption, in small amounts, will optimize digestion. Practice your race-day fueling plan during training to be fully prepared. Optional: Consume a swig of gel OR 1–3 energy chews/blocks after 60 minutes of riding.
Run	Option 1: Consume 2–3 sips of a sport drink at each aid station (~every 8–12 minutes). Option 2: Wear a hydration belt/pack and plan to consume 10 ounces of fluid, 80–100 calories and 400mg sodium (in the form of a sport drink) every 30 minutes of running. Take 1–2 sips every 8–10 minutes. Use aid stations for sipping/cooling with water. Option 3: Consume a swig of a gel before each aid station and wash down with water. Plan to finish one gel every 30–45 minutes of running.	Fueling and hydrating on the run can be challenging as it may not be comfortable and it's not always convenient to bring fluids with you. Although the race course will provide fluids at the aid stations, you need to train your stomach (in training sessions) to take in fluid and fuel while running. This may take up to 6 weeks. To hydrate frequently and conveniently, use a hydration belt/pack, especially when running longer than 45 minutes.

THREE

TRAINING FUNDAMENTALS

To maximize your triathlon training potential, your training must have structure and purpose. Otherwise, you risk injury or a performance plateau. Instead of thinking of your triathlon training as three separate sport disciplines (swimming, biking, and running), you must train for the demands of triathlon as one sport: swim-bike-run.

Triathlon training is both a science and an art. You can apply laboratory research to real-world settings to understand how to maximize performance. The art of training is managing your experience. Both are necessary for triathlon success. This chapter will give you an understanding of how to train for a triathlon, appropriate ways to measure your progress, and tips for effective season planning.

TRAINING PRINCIPLES

To improve fitness, your body needs to adapt to a certain amount of sport-specific training stress. Exercising is not necessarily training. As an athlete, you need to train in a purposeful, systematic way to achieve a performance goal. A well-designed triathlon training plan is designed to change your physiology to prepare for the demands of your upcoming event.

In addition to recovery, there are three main elements to consider within any well-built training program: frequency, duration, and intensity.

Frequency: Frequency is how often you train. Although training too hard or too often may bring diminishing returns, your body requires a specific amount of stress in order to adapt. Ideally, you should train each sport (swim, bike, and run) no fewer than three times per week.

Duration: Generally expressed in minutes or hours, duration can also be measured in distance. Whereas long workouts build endurance and strength, other workouts are of short duration—to promote recovery, for skill work, or to be performed at a high-intensity effort. Because there's no "right" amount of time to train each day, it's not about how long you train, but the quality of each training session.

Intensity: Intensity can be described as a level of physical effort. Although high-intensity is needed in your training plan, it's easy to train too hard, too often. Most athletes struggle to keep the easy sessions easy. To optimize training adaptations and provide different stimuli to your body, manipulating intensity is key.

There are many ways to organize your week of training; don't make the mistake of doing too much too soon. When a sport is new, you may find yourself wanting to train beyond what your training plan calls for (and what your body can handle). A typical mistake is skipping steps in order to speed up the process to develop a high level of fitness too early in your development. A patient approach to gaining fitness is critical, especially in the early stages of your triathlon journey when skill work is essential. Building a solid foundation and learning sport-specific skills take years to master. The most important aspect of training is to be consistent with frequency before increasing duration and intensity. Remember, the quality of your training is more important than the quantity of your training. Train smarter, not harder.

MEASURING PROGRESS

Innovative technologies have changed the way athletes train and race. Yet, at times, they can overcomplicate simple activities like going for a bike ride. Making a new gadget a useful training tool takes some knowledge.

RPE: Rating of perceived exertion is the most user-friendly (and inexpensive) way to understand how hard you are working. RPE is the best subjective indicator of intensity, giving you an honest self-assessment of how hard (or easy) you are working. Measuring RPE requires matching your effort to a number on a scale of 1 to 10: one being easy, six being somewhat hard, and ten being very hard. It's easy to underestimate your exertion level; don't let your ego get in the way of gauging your effort. With experience, you'll become better at determining your RPE.

Heart rate: Heart rate helps you understand your response to training. Typically, a performance test (cycling and/or running) establishes heart rate zones. Because your heart rate is your body's response to a dose of work, it neither provides immediate feedback nor quantifies training load. It's easy to chase the "perfect" number by going too hard or easing up. Your heart rate is also influenced by variables other than intensity, including weather, diet, hydration status, stress, and fatigue.

Power: Measured in watts, a power meter gives you immediate feedback on your work rate while riding your bike. Power meters are now available to measure your work output while running as well. A functional threshold test—a cycling test to determine your average power output over an hour—is one way to determine training zones. It's important to note that power meter data is only valuable if it's correctly interpreted and consistently monitored. Although power is an objective, reliable measure of intensity, power is influenced by fatigue, bike fit position, terrain, and brand of device.

Pace: Pacing is important, but it's a skill that comes from being exceptionally in tune with your body. The biggest issue with pace-based triathlon training and racing is this: You won't be able to predict the level of fatigue that you will experience from sport to sport. As a result, you may find yourself frustrated when you can't go as fast as you once did as a one-sport athlete.

Training Zones: RPE Reference

It's okay to use power and heart rate training zones, but RPE is a valuable tool with which you should become familiar. It's important to listen to your body when it comes to workout and racing execution.

Zone 1 (RPE 4/10): Easy

This is a very sustainable level of effort. It should feel ridiculously easy to hold good form. You can't go too easy, so be sure to enjoy it.

Zone 2 (RPE 5/10): Smooth

Although not as easy as Zone 1, this is a comfortable level of effort—one that you can maintain for several hours. You should be able to hold a conversation (full sentences) for the entire length of the workout.

Zone 3 (RPE 6–7/10): Steady

You can sustain this level of effort for a reasonable amount of time, but you may experience some fatigue and soreness from it. You shouldn't feel breathless, but conversation will be limited to simple and quick responses. Because you will feel like you are getting a great workout in this zone, many athletes fall into the trap of training in this zone for every workout. Why is it a trap? Because it's not easy enough to experience true aerobic benefits, and it's not hard enough to produce lactic acid from anaerobic glycolysis (breaking down glucose for energy).

Zone 4 (RPE 8–9/10): Strong

This zone is uncomfortable and requires great focus. Breathing is labored, and you can barely speak. Because of the intensity, this effort is usually reserved for high-intensity intervals of short duration. Go too hard in this zone for too long and you will experience great fatigue (which increases the risk for injury).

Zone 5 (RPE 10/10): Very Strong

This effort is extremely uncomfortable and is limited to only very short efforts. It's nearly impossible to speak a word at this effort. Because intervals at this effort are so short, it's likely that your mind will want to quit well before your body does.

HOW TO PLAN SEASONALLY

Periodization is a fancy term that refers to the big-picture plan for your triathlon training. Your training plan should account for your fitness ability, time availability, work and family demands, and race-day goals. By organizing your training and altering the frequency, intensity, and volume of your training sessions in cycles (or blocks), you can optimize physical and performance adaptations and minimize the potential for overstressing the body. Ultimately, this will allow you to develop different aspects of your fitness at different times of the year, helping you peak for your best performance when it matters the most.

Here's a sample of a 22-week periodized schedule for a sprint triathlon:

Off-season: rejuvenate the body and mind (3 weeks)

Prep phase: preparing to train, improving lifestyle habits, developing a structured routine (1 week)

Foundation building phase: working on skills, strength, and form/technique (6 weeks)

Building race fitness phase: strength and endurance focus (6 weeks)—this is a great time for a tune-up/practice race

Race-specific phase: race-type efforts and practicing transitions, nutrition, and pacing (4 weeks)

Taper and race week: reducing volume with a spice of intensity (1 week)

Race recovery: mentally and physically recover and rejuvenate (1 week)

Depending on the time of your next race, you may choose to return to the foundation building phase or race-specific phase of training.

When it comes to season planning, don't think of your training as preparing you for one race at a time. No athlete—not even an Olympic-caliber athlete—can maintain peak fitness all year long. You can only achieve peak fitness once or twice a year. It's very important to choose your races carefully. For example, practice/tune-up races give you the opportunity to test yourself before a more important race. They also give you race-day experience while reminding you that not every race needs to be a best-ever, personal record performance. Periodization ensures long-term improvements and longevity in sport, while helping you peak (physically, mentally, and emotionally) at the most appropriate times in your season.

REST, RECOVERY, AND INJURIES

Training for a triathlon is more intensive and time-consuming than training for a single sport, which means proper recovery is more important than ever. Completing a workout only creates the *potential* for fitness gains. In recovery, the body's adaptive process kicks in, enabling you to better handle future training stress, which allows for fitness improvements.

Your body is constantly trying to resist and manage stress. Unfortunately, your body doesn't know the difference between life stress (e.g., a sick child or a time-sensitive work deadline) and training stress (e.g., a fun 30-minute run workout with your friends). Although exercise can make you more resistant to sickness, too much stress of any sort can leave you run down, exhausted, and vulnerable to injury.

Sleep, diet, and other lifestyle choices all affect how your body recovers from a workout. To perform at an optimal level, maintaining excellent health (including mental, hormonal, and immune system health) is imperative.

Recovery from training is dependent on many factors. To optimize recovery, factor in the following:

- Previous and current workout type (sport, intensity, volume)
- Current nutritional status
- Current overall health status
- Lifestyle stress (sleep, work, family, relationship, travel)
- Mental status (stressed, anxious, depressed)
- Environment (hot, humid, cold, high altitude)

To help you perform well—and to keep your body in good health—you must embrace rest. Here are a few ways to take your recovery to the next level:

- **Get enough sleep.** Sleep is free and performance enhancing. Aim for 7–10 hours of restful sleep per night. Keep daytime naps less than 30 minutes.
- **Gift yourself a recharge day.** To promote healing and rejuvenation for the mind and body, take a day off from training and try to minimize life stressors.
- **Pay attention to diet and nutrition.** Avoid undereating or over-indulging between workouts. Prioritize a diet rich in a variety of nutrient-dense foods and always strive to eat "enough" to support your energy demands. The better you fuel and hydrate before and during a workout, the easier it is to keep your body in good hormonal (metabolic) health, while supporting the immune system. The quicker you recover today, the harder you can train tomorrow.
- **Enjoy active recovery.** Not every workout needs to boost fitness. Unlike a complete day off, actively moving blood at a very low intensity can help the muscles repair from previous damage.
- **Take advantage of recovery tools.** There are plenty of tools that can help expedite your recovery process: compression, foam rolling, Epsom salt, magnesium cream, active release therapy (ART), dry needling, meditation, yoga, massage, and warm/cold treatments. Despite having strong pain-killing properties, the use of NSAIDs (non-steroidal anti-inflammatory drugs) is not advised, as side effects of overuse (or long-term usage) include gastrointestinal (GI) complications, kidney failure, ulcers, hyponatremia, and stomach bleeding.

Staying Healthy

Daily exercise plays an important role in mental and physical health. Here are some tips for determining when to proceed with your planned workout, modify your training, or take a few days off.

Feeling sick?

- If symptoms are above the neck (e.g., sniffles, a headache), proceed with caution. Reduce training intensity and duration and let your body guide the workout.
- If symptoms are below the neck (e.g., coughing, fever, upset stomach, diarrhea), put all physical activity on hold until you feel back to normal. Because the immune system is compromised, training will not lead to positive adaptations.

Feeling a twinge?

- If pain exceeds a 3 on a 10-point scale, you can't take your mind off the twinge, or you can't maintain good form, stop the training session. If your issue doesn't improve in 5–7 days, consult with a medical professional.
- If pain is minimal and the twinge subsides after you warm up (i.e., after 10–15 minutes), proceed with awareness and caution. Reduce intensity and duration as needed. If the twinge doesn't improve (or gets worse) after 5–7 days, consult with a medical professional.

HOW TO PREVENT INJURIES

Training for an event requires great mental and physical preparation. Unfortunately, pushing your physical comfort zone may come at a cost. Some injuries or illnesses are not directly caused by a workout, but training may exacerbate an underlying issue—like hip tightness due to too much sitting or back pain due to poor posture at work. Although you may not be able to prevent an injury or illness, there are several ways to reduce your risk.

Whether you are a long-time athlete or just starting a structured training program, consider the following that may place you at risk for a physical setback:

- Inconsistent training
- Poor recovery habits
- Training too hard
- Little time spent warming up
- Minimal/no strength training
- Muscle imbalances or weaknesses
- Ignoring an injury/ache
- New/different training environment or road surface (e.g., trails, hills)
- New/different equipment/gear (e.g., shoes)
- Poor posture/tightness
- Restless sleep
- Stress
- Haphazard eating habits
- Underfueling
- Dehydration
- Pushing through extreme fatigue
- Frequent travel
- Overtraining (increasing training duration/intensity too quickly)
- Underlying health issues

As an athlete, it's your responsibility to be an active participant in all aspects of your life. You must always use your best judgment with your training—and remind yourself that your lifestyle choices impact your training. Athletic success is built on great mind-body awareness.

ADDRESSING COMMON INJURIES

Injuries could be due to training volume, overuse, and movement patterns. Here are a few of the most common injuries and suggestions for addressing them.

Swimmer's Shoulder: Swimming puts your shoulder joint through a lot of motion. Most shoulder issues result from overuse, stroke mechanics, lack of mobility, and fatigue. Swimming through pain only increases inflammation and damage to the joint and surrounding tendons. Improve your posture, rest your shoulder, and work with a physical therapist to strengthen the rotator cuff muscles. When healed, have an experienced triathlon swim coach analyze your swimming form.

Sciatica: The sciatic nerve runs the length of the lower back, through the buttocks, and down into the lower leg. Sciatica causes pain, numbness, and tingling. Triggers include age-related changes in the spine, weak glutes, and poor posture. Symptoms resemble a herniated disc, bursitis, or piriformis syndrome. Consult with a physical therapist to help restore normal range of motion, assess muscle recruitment patterns, improve pelvic control, and improve motor patterns.

Plantar Fasciitis: A thick band of connective tissue, called the plantar fascia, extends from the heel bone to the toes. Through use and overuse, common during training, micro-tears can develop and the plantar fascia can become inflamed. An extreme change in training (or terrain), poor foot biomechanics, improper shoe choice, flat feet, or a weak foot arch can overstretch or tear the plantar fascia. Heel pain is the most common symptom, especially first thing in the morning. Common modes of treatment include foot, Achilles tendon, and calf strengthening, wearing a night splint, avoiding barefoot walking, and soft tissue massage or release.

Iliotibial Band Syndrome (ITBS): Along the outside of your thigh runs the iliotibial band, a long, narrow band of fascia. ITBS often feels like a sharp pain on the bony outside of the knee. A common injury in runners, ITBS can also affect cyclists— due to an increase in training volume or intensity, or a change in your bike fit, cleat position, or saddle position. Physical therapy can help improve hip range of motion, strengthen the hip and glute muscles, and improve core strength. Athletes may also experience relief through dry needling, active release therapy, and soft-tissue massage.

Stress fracture: When muscles become fatigued and can no longer absorb the added shock of training, a bone can become stressed, causing tiny cracks. This eventually results in a stress reaction or fracture. Stress fractures occur primarily in weight-bearing bones, such as the pelvis (neck of femur), lower leg, and foot. Individuals with an energy deficiency due to inadequate nutrition intake, an eating disorder, amenorrhea (infrequent menstrual cycle), and loss of bone mineral density (osteopenia) are at great risk. Localized pain with activity is the most common symptom. An MRI is the most sensitive test for diagnosis. A bone may require 6–12 weeks to heal, whereas rehab may require an additional 3–6 months. Treatment includes complete rest from weight-bearing activities to ensure complete healing. When the stress fracture is healed, it's important to gradually build up mileage to avoid a re-injury and to continue with physical therapy and strength training. Due to the magnitude of this type of injury, a team approach to treatment—with a sports doctor, physical therapist, sports dietitian, and psychologist—is advised.

FOUR

SWIMMING

Triathlon swimming is different than competitive pool swimming. Bad stroke habits in the pool will come at a cost in the open water. Recognizing the challenges of the open water triathlon swim (e.g., crowds, rough or murky water), your swim training should emphasize technique, strength, and power.

In a triathlon event, the swim is generally the shortest discipline. Swim distances typically range from 400 yards (sprint) to 2.4 miles (Ironman). Although you will only be in the water for 10 to 20 percent of your race time (e.g., 10 to 90 minutes), don't assume that your swim training should take up little time in your weekly training schedule. Insufficient swim training uses up valuable energy on race day—energy that could be used for the bike and run. Swimming may not be the most logistically accessible sport, but you may need to spend more than 20 percent of your weekly training volume in the pool. To stay motivated, view your swim training as an exciting new challenge.

FUNDAMENTALS

If you lack a swimming background, you may notice that your current fitness level doesn't translate easily to swimming. Unlike the experienced swimmer with their fishlike ability to slice through the water, if you are inexperienced and try to swim fast, you'll quickly feel out of breath. And because improvements are slow to make in this technique-driven sport, swim training can feel discouraging.

Even if you are in excellent physical shape, water resistance makes swimming physically exhausting. Just imagine biking or running into extreme headwinds! To swim forward, you must pull water backward. This requires a lot of energy, strength, and power from your upper body. Additionally, unlike on land, where you've learned to work against gravity since you were a baby, gravity is no longer a factor in the water. Learning how to hold your body in the water, while minimizing drag, can be extremely difficult to master. But it's a necessary skill to reduce the energy cost of swimming. Once you feel comfortable keeping your face in the water, you need to learn how and when to breathe. Because swimming is a skill-focused sport, you must dedicate a lot of time, energy, and patience to improving your technique. Maybe that's why competitive swimmers refer to swim training as swimming "practice."

The most basic swimming skill to master is holding your body position. On land, you have great body awareness when it comes to movement. But once you submerge yourself into the water, most of your body weight is dispersed. It can take a while to get used to feeling weightless in the water.

Proper body position will help you move forward in the water with minimal energy wasted. By learning how to keep your head, hips, and feet in a straight line, you'll create less drag. Although your lungs give the upper body natural buoyancy, you need to learn how to "hold up" your hips and legs. Sinking legs means more mass to move through the water. Excessively kicking to overcome drag wastes a lot of energy.

Most of your propulsive force comes from the upper body; a powerful catch and pull moves you forward. By catching (or holding) the water with the fingers, hand, forearm, and upper body, you are literally grabbing the water and pulling yourself forward. A high (but efficient) stroke rate is key for open water swimming. Proper body position and alignment will help reduce drag, while your hips and legs play an important role in propulsion. When timed appropriately with your stroke, hip movement can contribute to overall power. Although forceful kicking offers little return on investment regarding propulsion, trying to power through the water with only your arms is not the most economical way to swim. When you kick, keep your feet relaxed and pointing away from you (not toward the bottom of the pool). Avoid scissor kicking (crossing your legs), as this can throw your body out of alignment. Kick timing is key. A two-, four-, or six-beat kick pattern will help drive your momentum forward. As for moving through the water, your body—shoulder, torso, and hips—should cooperatively roll throughout each stroke.

Before you try to swim faster or longer, do yourself a big favor and spend a significant amount of time improving your body posture and stroke mechanics in the pool.

CORRECT

INCORRECT

Form

There are four phases of the swim stroke: catch, pull, exit, and recovery.

Catch and Pull: The catch starts immediately after the recovery phase. Extend your arm forward by making your back feel wide, like you are wrapping your arms around a large exercise stability ball. Your shoulders should roll slightly forward. Engage your upper back muscles, which are a strong muscle group designed for powerful swimming. While holding this position, your outstretched arm will enter the water, starting with your thumb and pointer finger. Keep a slight spread between your fingers. Your hand and forearm are now your paddle. Without dropping your elbow, move your arm through the water, feeling the water's pressure on your palm and forearm. Your forearm should feel like it's holding and moving that exercise ball through the water. If your elbow drops, you will lose the tension of the water against your hand and won't have anything to hold onto to move you forward. Avoid crossing the midline of the body during your catch. To generate propulsion and to avoid sinking hips and legs, don't pause or glide with each stroke. Efficient swimming is rhythmic and fluid.

Exit: Your hand and arm are now leaving the water. Your core should stay tight, as if you were holding a plank position on the floor. Because great acceleration comes from this phase, continue to hold the water from the catch phase, just past your hips. Your hand should exit by your thigh with force. Instead of rotating just with your hips, you should feel like you are rolling slightly with your shoulders, torso, and hips, moving your hip slightly out of the way as your hand exits the water. During this time, the other hip will drive forward. This forward hip drive, along with rhythmic kicking and slight rotation, helps with propulsion. Swimming with a flat body position places a tremendous amount of strain on the shoulders.

Recovery: The beginning of the stroke cycle starts once your arm is out of the water. This phase should cost little energy. Lifting your elbow to drag your fingertips above the water requires a lot of energy. Therefore, keep a straighter arm and simply throw your arm over the water to initiate the catch phase. Your stroke doesn't need to look graceful above the water. Underwater is where all the action happens.

Breathing While Swimming

Feeling out of breath while swimming? The struggle is real.

Trying to both exhale and inhale when your face is out of the water is counterproductive. Before you turn your head to take a breath, exhale forcefully through your mouth and nose when your head is in the water, as if you were blowing out a dozen birthday candles. When you turn your head to breathe, you'll find it easier to take in air without gasping.

Although swimming freestyle has many moving parts, breathing should be rhythmic and timed with your stroke. As one arm is extended in front of you, you'll breathe to the other side by slightly turning your head (not your entire body) so that your chin is near your shoulder.

You'll likely have a preferred side for breathing, but learning how to breathe to both sides can help in choppy open water or if the sun is getting in your eyes. More importantly, many upper-body aches due to stroke flaws—like crossing your arms over the midline of the body, scissor kicking, and a sinking outstretched arm—develop when you only breathe to one side.

Terrain

As a triathlete, it's important to think like an open water swimmer. But before you jump into the big blue sea, master your technique in the safe and controlled environment of a swimming pool. Luckily, there are several ways to simulate open water skills in a pool setting.

For example, practicing sighting can help strengthen your neck muscles for the open water. Swimming in one lane with 3–4 people abreast can reduce anxiety when swimming in a crowd. Treading water to start a lap (instead of pushing off the wall) can teach you how to quickly build momentum as you would at the start of a race. If you have access to a pool without lane lines (which are used to reduce turbulence), practice swimming in a straight line without using the black line as a guide.

Because an elevated heart rate can cause breathing issues during the triathlon swim, try "deck-ups." For this drill, you will swim one or two fast laps, quickly push yourself up and out of the water, touch an object (like a wall or chair) a few feet away, and then carefully jump (or slide) back into the pool to swim another one or two laps, controlling your breathing in the process.

Although training in a pool will help you get to the level of fitness that triathlon swimming demands, open water swimming requires a special set of mental and physical skills—skills that can only be achieved by swimming in open water. You need to be familiar with the kinds of conditions you are likely to encounter on race day, at a similar intensity, and for a similar distance. To reduce your open water fears and swim to your fitness capabilities, get familiar with the conditions (including water temperature) you are likely to experience on race day. Practice sighting, staying on course, and managing the unpredictable nature of the open water as you swim at different intensities surrounded by other people.

Open Water Swimming: 5 Pro Tips

1. Review the course. Take notice of the water movement. Make note of the sighting buoys, particularly the turn buoys. Look for landmarks like a brightly colored building, cellphone tower, flagpole, or large tree to help you navigate the open water and stay on course.

2. The shock of cold water can cause your lungs to contract, causing hyperventilation. Before you take your first stroke, go waist deep, submerge your face in the water, and blow bubbles until your breathing is controlled.

3. Use a copious amount of Vaseline or anti-chafing cream around your ankles, arms, neckline, and back to minimize chafing.

4. Don't ruin your swim by skipping the warm-up. Spend 10–15 minutes on dry land and then in the water to promote blood flow and elevate the heart rate. During this time, you can also adjust your swimsuit/wetsuit, cap, and goggles.

5. Aerophagia, or the act of ingesting air while swimming, can cause gas, stomach cramping, or belching. Avoid starting out too hard, breathe every other stroke, and forcefully exhale through your nose and mouth when your face is in the water.

GEAR

If you come from a swimming background, you probably own a lot of swim gear. As a three-sport athlete, the list of essential (and desired) gear can get rather long (and pricey). Luckily, triathlon swimming only requires a few essential items, such as a swimsuit, swim cap, and goggles.

Suit: Choose a competitive swimsuit to reduce friction and drag in the water. When the water temperature is below 76.1 degrees Fahrenheit (24.5° C), you are allowed to wear a wetsuit during the triathlon swim. In addition to keeping you warmer than in a swimsuit, a wetsuit offers buoyancy, compression, and speed.

Wetsuits come in two styles: full and sleeveless. A full sleeve wetsuit will be the most buoyant (and warmest) option, whereas a sleeveless wetsuit may provide more shoulder rotation and less sensation of constriction. To find the one that fits your body shape, try on wetsuits from several brands. Most wetsuit companies allow returns or exchanges within 30 days of purchase. As far as fit goes, a wetsuit should be tight, but not restrictive, around the chest and shoulders. Keep in mind that neoprene will stretch in the water. Although you may not need a top-of-the-line wetsuit, a quality triathlon wetsuit is advised.

Swim cap: Because swim caps come in different sizes and types (e.g., latex or silicone), find one that provides a secure fit while you swim.

Goggles: Because open water swimming requires you to lift your eyes out of the water (often into the sun) to "sight" the shore, landmarks, boats, or buoys, invest in a few different pairs of goggles. Goggles with wider (or curved) lenses will have increased field of vision. It may take trying a few different models to find the perfect pair. A good pair of goggles shouldn't leak or fog after one use.

Swimming equipment: Invest in a variety of tools to help with swimming technique. A pull buoy, ankle lock/strap, snorkel, fins, buoyancy shorts, and paddles can be used to help correct technique flaws while reinforcing swimming position, alignment, and tautness.

Swimming Gear Checklist

- ❏ Swimsuit: $40–60
- ❏ Goggles: $10–30
- ❏ Swim cap: $2–8
- ❏ Wetsuit (optional): $200–600
- ❏ Pool equipment (optional): $50–100

FIVE

CYCLING

Sandwiched between the swim and run, the bike portion of the triathlon is the longest discipline in both time and distance. With nearly half of your race time spent on two wheels, insufficient skills and not enough time in the saddle will cost you valuable time and energy on race day. Proper bike training will not only help you get faster, but also minimize the effect of cycling on your running legs.

When it comes to triathlon gear and equipment, cycling is by far the most expensive discipline. Plus, training outdoors has its hazards, especially when you are sharing the road with cars, pedestrians, and nature. For these reasons, many triathletes don't train properly, or spend a considerable amount of time cycling indoors. At the end of the day, preparation for the bike portion of a triathlon is about having the right equipment, doing the right training, and constantly working to improve your bike handling skills and terrain management.

FUNDAMENTALS

Cycling culture may look intimidating, but as long as you are riding a bike and having fun, you are part of the club. Building basic bike fitness is fairly straightforward: Go ride your bike. However, to truly showcase your cycling fitness, proper bike handling skills and terrain management are critical for safety, confidence, and efficiency. Knowing how to descend, brake, corner, stand, climb, and change your gears will take your bike fitness to an entirely new level. For most triathletes, due to too much indoor riding (or dislike of bike riding), these fundamental skills are lacking. For example, going downhill on a bicycle at 40+ mph is a pure adrenaline rush—as long as you can safely handle your bike at these speeds. Let's look into a few important bike-handling skills and how you can improve your confidence on two wheels.

Descending: Position yourself a bit back on the saddle. You don't want to brake the whole way down the hill, as it puts tension on your arms and hands, prevents the wheel from moving freely, and may overheat your brake pads. If you find yourself going faster than your comfort level, or when approaching a sharp turn, brake softly and then let it go. Practice on a small hill with a slight decline. As you gain more confidence and trust in your skills, work your way up to longer hills, where you'll pick up speed. Eventually, practice descending on a road with sweeping turns.

Braking: For your safety, it's critical to practice your braking abilities before you find yourself in an emergency situation. To avoid an "over the bars" crash, pay attention to how to use each brake. Most importantly, master the use of your front brake (on your left handlebar). Because some brakes are more sensitive than others, you need to know the "feel" of the brakes on your bike. Find an empty parking lot and ride fast for 10 seconds. Then come to a controlled stop by a designated spot on the road. This will give you a better sense of your bike's braking power and the time it takes you to come to a complete stop from a fast speed.

Cornering: Making turns (especially tight U-turns around a cone) is a necessary skill to master. Always look ahead to avoid grease, painted lines, sand, or rocks—especially in the rain. These road obstacles can make your wheels unstable. Complete your breaking before the turn. Avoid braking during the turn, which causes your bike to lose traction. As you turn, keep the inside pedal up, the outside pedal down, and your weight on the outside foot. You can even move your butt slightly off the saddle to put more weight on the outside pedal. Counter-steer by leaning the bike—not your body—into the turn. Push your hand on the side of the handlebar where you want to turn. Always look in the direction you want to go to maintain your line. To avoid feeling unstable in a tight turn, start at the outside and carve a smooth arc through the apex of the turn. As you come out of the turn, straighten the bike and begin pedaling. Always shift into a lighter gear before the turn so that you can quickly regain momentum out of the turn (the same tip applies for stopping).

Bike handling: Lastly, although it seems basic, you must learn how to signal a turn, point to something in the road, and take in nutrition (from a bottle or your pocket) as you ride. All of these tasks require you to ride your bike with only one hand. The only way to become efficient at this skill is to practice. In an empty parking lot, practice lifting one hand at a time off the handlebars to learn how to balance yourself on your bike. Then practice grabbing your water bottle from the cage and looking behind you as if you were about to make a signal or turn.

Cycling Skills: 5 Pro Tips

1. For smoother shifting, braking, and turning, anticipation is key. For example, change your gears right before you really need to, especially when approaching a hill.

2. Always ride with a bike and flat-tire repair kit. Don't wait until you are on the side of the road to perfect your flat-changing skills.

3. Learn the rules of riding on the road. Know how to signal appropriately when making a turn or pointing out a hazard on the road. Try to anticipate the decisions of the drivers around you.

4. Check your bike (cables, brakes, tires, spokes, chain, etc.) before every ride. Don't forget to pump your tires. The recommended tire pressure can be found on the sidewall of your tire. Give your bike a quick clean after every ride.

5. In wet weather, stay off the painted line, watch out for oil, and brake earlier than usual, especially when taking a turn. Look far enough ahead that you can see and react to any obstacles on the road or on the shoulder.

Form

Like a good pair of running shoes, having a proper bike fit can make for a more enjoyable cycling experience. A professional fitter will consider the correct seat height, tilt and position, crank size, handlebar height, arm cups/elbow pads, and cleat position to optimize both your biomechanics and aerodynamics. A bike that is not your size (or is improperly adjusted) increases the risk for injury—not to mention making for an uncomfortable ride. Although a costly investment, a bike fit is worth the time, effort, and money.

Knowing what you need from a bike fit is crucial. Aerodynamics are important, however, your optimal position will likely develop and evolve over time. As a beginner, it's not practical to prioritize aerodynamics at the cost of comfort. At your first bike fit, athletic comfort and injury prevention are top priorities. The proper saddle position and type will ensure appropriate pelvic rotation, soft tissue clearance, and support, while maximizing power. This position will likely be the most aerodynamic position for your current riding ability. To optimize time-trial position, the aerobars will need to be adjusted so you can execute the best aero technique (shoulder shrug and head tuck) for your body. Supporting the elbows and hands will ensure aerodynamic efficiency and comfort. Proper crank length will open the hip angle, making it easier to bring the knee over the top of the stroke. An incorrect crank arm size can result in knee, foot, ankle, and hip pain, as well as saddle sores. Although your bike fitter can put you into an ideal position, you must constantly work on maintaining this position for extended periods of time. Although a new bike position may take time to get used to, you should never be in pain when riding your bike.

Pedaling in a circle may look simple, but it's actually quite complex. Mobility, flexibility, past and current limiters (i.e., injuries), and an improper bike fit can affect your pedaling mechanics. Plus, pedaling with clipless pedals isn't the same as pedaling with the platform pedals that you used as a kid. When pedaling, most triathletes make the mistake of pushing down and then pulling up (box-like), which is highly inefficient. Instead, to get the most power from each crank revolution, the most efficient pedaling is in a circle—feeling constant tension on the chain throughout the entire pedal stroke. Pedaling should be smooth, without any dead spots (clicking) in your pedal stroke. Single leg drills and knowing how to change your gears appropriately can improve the efficiency of your pedal stroke.

Terrain

Time in the saddle is the first step in building your cycling fitness, and indoor bike training is an extremely time-effective, efficient, and safe way to accomplish this. Although a stationary spin bike at your local gym may look like a suitable way to build bike fitness, it's best to train on your primary race bike (triathlon or road), which is properly fit to your body. Otherwise, there's potential for lower back, neck, shoulder, and knee injuries from attempting to train on a bike that's not in the proper position for your body and riding style. With so many indoor bike trainers on the market, riding in the comfort of your own home, on your own racing bike, has never been more enjoyable (or affordable).

One popular indoor trainer is the direct-drive trainer, which attaches to your rear wheel dropout (drive train). By removing the rear wheel, you don't have to worry about replacing your tire as regularly as you would with friction trainers. Plus, a direct-drive trainer provides a quiet and smooth ride. There's also the friction trainer, which places a small roller against the rear wheel while utilizing magnetic or fluid resistance. Today, many trainers are "smart," which means they communicate wirelessly to a third-party training app (or virtual riding world) to control resistance and guide you through power-based intervals. With such a controlled environment, you can also work at different cadences, nail specific intervals, and practice your pedaling technique without the interruption of lights and turns—not to mention the many curveballs thrown by Mother Nature or distracted drivers.

Although there are many positive aspects of indoor trainer riding, one of the greatest benefits of riding outside is learning how to properly use your gears.

Changing Gears

Not knowing how or when to shift your gears can cause you to lose momentum, drop your chain off the chainring, or struggle to get to the top of a steep hill. To shift properly, you need to know how to shift to the right gear before you need it, allowing you to maintain a smooth and efficient pedal stroke.

For a big shift (e.g., up or down a hill), you'll switch between the front chainrings. The left shifter controls the front derailleur. In simple terms, the small chainring makes pedaling easier (for uphill), while moving to the big chainring will let you pedal harder (for downhill). Before approaching a major terrain change, anticipate what shifting needs to happen and give yourself time to get into the right gear.

For smaller shifts in the wind, undulating terrain, or for more efficient riding, the shifting mechanism on the right side of your handlebars will move the chain up and down the rear cassette (right side of the back wheel). The right shifter controls the rear derailleur. Moving the chain up the cogs will make pedaling easier while moving the chain down will make pedaling harder.

Don't settle into being a one-gear rider. In an empty parking lot, practice shifting from your big to your small chainring and moving your chain up and down your rear cassette. Notice how this affects your effort and cadence (number of pedaling revolutions per minute). A simple trick to prevent your chain from dropping when moving from the big to small chainring (and vice versa) is to first make sure your chain is in the middle of the rear cassette by making small shifts with the right shifter. In order to master this skill, you must practice changing your gears in outdoor settings.

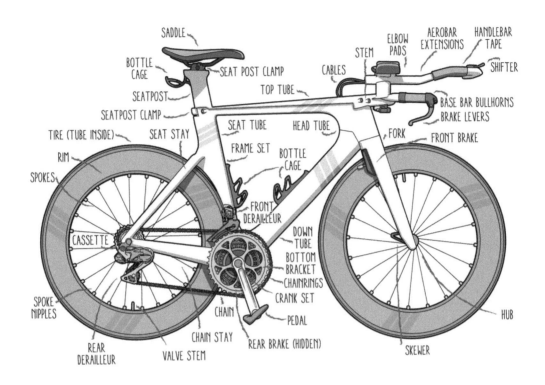

SADDLE

BOTTLE CAGE

SEAT POST CLAMP

SEATPOST

TOP TUBE

SEATPOST CLAMP

CABLES

STEM

ELBOW PADS

AEROBAR EXTENSIONS

HANDLEBAR TAPE

SHIFTER

TIRE (TUBE INSIDE)

SEAT STAY

SEAT TUBE

HEAD TUBE

FRAME SET

RIM

BOTTLE CAGE

FORK

BASE BAR BULLHORNS

BRAKE LEVERS

FRONT BRAKE

SPOKES

FRONT DERAILLEUR

CASSETTE

DOWN TUBE

BOTTOM BRACKET

CHAINRINGS

CRANK SET

SPOKE NIPPLES

CHAIN

PEDAL

HUB

REAR DERAILLEUR

VALVE STEM

CHAIN STAY

REAR BRAKE (HIDDEN)

SKEWER

GEAR

As a newbie triathlete, the improvements you make in fitness will impact your performance more than an expensive set of race wheels, an aero helmet, or high-end bike components. That being said, having the essentials will certainly make triathlon bike training much easier.

Bike: You may have noticed that a triathlon bike looks very different than a traditional road or hybrid bicycle. The major difference is the geometry of the frame and handlebar set-up. A road bike is typically light, stiff, and responsive. Equipped with drop bars, this allows you to make use of multiple hand positions, which makes for more comfortable climbing and descending. Easy to handle, a road bike also makes it fun to enjoy a casual ride and to constantly work on your bike-handling skills.

A triathlon bike puts you in a more compact, forward, aerodynamic position, reducing drag and letting you apply more direct transfer of power to the crank. This position also lessens the load on your quadriceps to ensure more efficient running off the bike. Built for speed in a straight line, a triathlon bike handles very differently than a road bike. It's not uncommon for beginner triathletes to feel unstable on a tri-bike compared to a road bike.

Purchasing a bike is a big investment, but your first bike likely won't be your forever bike. Buying from your local bike shop or triathlon store will help you find the right bike size for your body and budget. Plus, a new bike comes with a warranty and may even come with a service package. For beginners, consider investing in a road bike and install clip-on aerobars. Aerobars allow you to rest your elbows on pads to lower your body in a more aerodynamic (tucked) position. Although an aluminum bike frame is durable (and cost effective), carbon fiber is light, which makes for a smoother ride when on the road. Electrical shifting, while quite a pricey upgrade, allows you to change your gears with the push of a button instead of using conventional shift levers and mechanical cables. Not only is electronic shifting quick and precise but you can also shift better under a heavy load—like pedaling uphill or when standing out of the saddle.

You may also want to consider disc brakes (over rim brakes), which have more responsive and stronger braking power and control, especially in wet conditions. Regardless of the bike you choose, you need to understand the inner workings of your bike and take care of it. A clean bike is a happy machine.

Helmet: The best helmet for you is the one that best fits your head. To test for the proper fit, a helmet should stay in place unbuckled on your head when you turn your head upside down and moderately shake it. Helmets should be replaced every 5–10 years, as well as immediately after a crash. Visit https://www.helmet.beam.vt.edu/ for helmet ratings.

Clothing: Select cycling shorts (or bibs) based on the chamois, which is the padding inside the shorts, designed to protect your sensitive areas from road vibrations. For your jersey, choose polyester fabric to provide breathability and to wick moisture away from your body. Higher priced jerseys provide more panels of fabric, which may provide a better overall fit to your upper body. The jersey should be snug enough to help decrease drag. Consider brightly colored clothing for riding outdoors. You'll also need sunglasses to protect you from the bright sun and shield your eyes from debris. Worn for both the bike and run, select a pair based on comfort, durability, functionality, and style. Don't forget to purchase chamois cream for sensitive areas to eliminate friction between skin and clothing.

Clipless pedals and cycling shoes (optional): Keep your feet in place to improve pedaling efficiency and bike handling. Give yourself some time in an empty parking lot to learn how to practice clipping in and out.

Bike repair kit: In your kit you should have, at minimum: a multi-tool, CO2 inflator and cartridges (at least two), patch kit, spare tube, tire levers, and a $20 bill (in case you need to buy something when you are out on the road).

Extra goods: Don't forget to purchase a floor pump, cycling computer, water bottle cages (and water bottles), and rear/front bike lights.

Cycling Gear Checklist

- ❏ Bike: Road bikes range from $500–2000, triathlon bikes from $1500–10,000+.
- ❏ Bike fit: $225–300
- ❏ Helmet: $40–60
- ❏ Cycling shorts (or bibs): $90
- ❏ Cycling jersey: $60
- ❏ Chamois cream: $10–15
- ❏ Clipless pedals and cycling shoes: $75–250+
- ❏ Rear and front light: $40
- ❏ Bike repair kit: $35
- ❏ Floor pump: $20
- ❏ Cycling computer: $45
- ❏ Water bottle cage: $6
- ❏ Water bottle: $6–8
- ❏ Sunglasses: $80–$300
- ❏ Indoor bike trainer (optional): $150–1200

SIX

RUNNING

Although you've undoubt-edly run at some point in your life, triathlon running is very different than running as a standalone exercise. During a triathlon, by the time your feet hit the pavement, nearly 70 percent of your race is already complete. As a triathlete, the swim and bike will exhaust your body, making your legs feel like heavy bricks by the time you start running. It's not uncommon for your normal running mechanics to change due to fatigue. Oh, and there's also the physical and mental struggle of having to run with depleted energy stores.

Compared to running with fresh legs, most triathletes run 5 to 10 percent slower off the bike. To properly prepare for a triathlon, you can't train like a distance runner or track sprinter. Even if you are already an experienced runner, transitioning to triathlon may not be an easy adjustment—mentally or physically—but with the right training, you can feel excited and confident on race day.

FUNDAMENTALS

Becoming a better triathlon runner is much more than training for speed or distance, or accumulating weekly running miles. Proper run training means thinking like a triathlete—not like a runner.

One of the most important physiological components of successful triathlon running is resiliency. The stronger and more efficient you are, the easier it is to run well under fatigue. Training to improve your 5K or half-marathon times in a road race will not guarantee that you will become a faster runner off the bike. In fact, historically, most of the top triathletes lack a background in competitive running. Some elite triathletes can run faster off the bike relative to their own stand-alone run times! Not surprisingly, triathletes with a strong background in cycling tend to fare better running off the bike than their competitors.

There are four main areas that will help you become a better triathlon runner. Each is equally important. In fact, it's pretty unlikely that your running will improve if you master one without the others.

1. **Master easy, efficient running.** After swimming and biking, your body is fatigued. Being able to maintain good technique under fatigue is a critical component of keeping your momentum with good form. Running easy (or slow) is one of the best ways to become a more efficient runner—to increase your running economy. A decrease in running economy is often linked to dehydration, glycogen depletion, a decline in neurological muscle activity, and muscle damage. Thankfully, training can improve running economy.

   Most athletes spend much of their workouts running around 70 to 80 percent intensity. This "tempo" effort isn't bad, it's just not productive if you do it all the time. Why? Because at that pace, you are too fatigued to adapt to high-intensity training, and your heart rate is too high to condition the aerobic system. Because you can't improve what you don't train, easy runs are a great way to help your body utilize the fat metabolic pathway more efficiently, fine-tune your bio-mechanics, minimize overall cardio stress, reduce the load on your joints and muscles, and improve breathing techniques. All of this will help you run more consistently over time.

2. **Improve swimming and cycling.** Most stand-alone distance runners begin a race in the early morning, with a well-fueled and hydrated body and freshly tapered (rested) legs. An elite marathon runner can cover 26.2 miles in less than 2 hours and 20 minutes. A top professional Ironman athlete covers 26.2 miles in less than 2 hours and 55 minutes. Without a doubt, what precedes the run greatly impacts run performance. To become a better runner off the bike, the answer is not harder running or longer running, but being consistent with your running (and staying injury-free) as you train to become a stronger cyclist and open water swimmer.

3. **Strength train.** Triathlon is a strength-endurance sport. The more power you can generate with each stride, the faster you can run. The stronger your glutes, core, and lower legs, the longer you can generate that power with good form. Because of the corrosive nature of running, there's great risk for injury when you chase running miles or paces. Bricks, progressive efforts, easy efforts, double run days, hills, endurance efforts, soft impact runs, and treadmill running can help you become a better triathlon runner.

4. **Practice proper fueling and hydration.** Dehydration and glycogen depletion severely impair your running ability, especially in hot environments. Dehydration not only affects the pumping capacity of the heart, but it increases the rate of glycogen breakdown in the muscles. When your body runs low on glycogen (the primary fuel for the muscles and brain), you feel fatigued and often dizzy. While in a state of hypoglycemia, your body begins to break down muscle tissue for "fuel"—a process that not only suppresses the immune system but also contributes to a decline in muscle mass. Learning how to take in calories, electrolytes, and fluids in training keeps your body functioning well—this is also a critical component of successful triathlon racing.

Form

When you are in the early part of a workout or race, it's easy to hold good running form. But when fatigue sets in, your running technique will quickly fall apart. Your posture slumps, cadence slows, and stride length increases. You also lose communication with your glutes and hamstrings, which comprise your posterior chain—the muscles that help your leg propel you forward after your foot hits the ground. Not only that, but the oxygen cost of running increases, making it more exhausting to run. It's no surprise that so many triathletes shuffle (or walk) en route to the finish line.

To prevent these breakdowns from happening, always focus on your running mechanics. Form over pace. Identifying and correcting your individual biomechanical flaws will help you move with optimal mechanical efficiency, while also mitigating some of the injury risks that occur under fatigue.

Every runner has an innate running style, but there's always room to improve run economy. Make it your intention to always run with good running form.

Pre-run

1. Look slightly in front of you.

2. Stand tall with a long spine and tight core.

3. Relax your shoulders.

4. Your torso should be slightly in front of your hips.

5. Your knees should be in line with the middle of your foot, so that when you strike the ground with your foot, it's right under your hips.

6. Engage your glutes to hold your pelvis level and steady. Avoid an excessive anterior pelvic tilt.

7. Position your arms at a 90-degree angle, close to your sides.

8. Keep your hands in a relaxed fist, like you are holding a potato chip between your index finger and thumb.

9. Start marching forward while keeping tips 1-8 in mind.

During the run

1. Lean slightly forward.

2. Breathe from your belly (not your chest).

3. Fire your glutes to prevent your hip(s) from dropping. Make sure your knees are not collapsing inward.

4. Do a shoulder shrug (shoulders to ears) and then drop your shoulders as low as possible to relax your upper body.

5. Make sure your arms are not crossing the midline of your body.

6. Quicken your cadence to soften your foot strike and prevent overstriding.

Run Training: 5 Pro Tips

1. Don't be afraid to run easy. During an easy run, you should be able to hold a conversation without getting out of breath.

2. Learn to increase your running cadence to improve efficiency and to avoid over-striding. Although the recommended running cadence is somewhere around 180 steps per minute, every runner has their own innate running style. Anytime you attempt to change your run form, focus on making small adjustments while maintaining smooth rhythm with your stride.

3. Before a stand-alone run, dedicate at least 5–10 minutes to mobility, glute strength, and active stretching. An active warm-up will improve range of motion and improve body awareness of movement patterns.

4. Incorporate walk (or reset) breaks into your running to reduce fatigue, lessen muscle damage, provide a mental recharge, and fine-tune motor patterns. Walking is not failing to run.

5. Learn how to take in nutrition (e.g., sports drinks) while you are running. Consider the use of a hydration belt or pack to keep your arms moving freely when you run.

Terrain

Different terrains affect your running form, pace, and tactics. Although most triathlon runs take place on asphalt or concrete, it's beneficial to train on a variety of surfaces.

Because of its convenience and ability to generate speed, you'll likely spend much of your outdoor running time on a hard road surface. To reduce stress on bones and joints, asphalt is better than concrete. Red clay and packed dirt trails have an optimal amount of hardness and softness to absorb the impact of your body weight. Trails with tree roots and rocks can be very demanding and technical. Grass provides a soft surface, offering an extra layer of cushion for your joints, but it can hide holes and uneven surfaces. Be careful not to twist an ankle or injure yourself in a fall. Loose sand may be soft, but it can be tough on the lower leg muscles and joints. Sand is harder when wet, so running closer to the water may provide a safer surface. Most runners love the soft and spongy surface of the track for speed workouts. However, approach the track with caution. Not only are you more likely to run at a higher intensity than you normally would on the road, but repetitively circling around the same tight loop (in the same direction) can increase the risk of lower leg injuries.

Don't be afraid of running on hilly terrain. Compared to flat surfaces, hills make for an effective training tool because they promote more economical running form when your heart rate is elevated. That said, because impact forces are much higher when running downhill, it's best to slowly acclimate to this unnatural type of pounding. The best type of hills to train on are between 3 to 8 percent incline and should not take more than 30 seconds to 3 minutes to run up (or down). If hills aren't available in your neck of the woods, seek out a treadmill for a quality hill training session.

The treadmill may look like a boring way to run but it's actually a valuable training tool—one that allows you to build your mental strength while controlling the specificity of your workout. And because the treadmill belt is smooth and cushioned, it can be more forgiving on your joints, especially for an easy run. Research shows that when you set the treadmill on a 1 percent incline, it closely simulates the energy cost of outdoor running. By increasing the incline even more, you can simulate different types of hills. Some treadmills are even equipped with a decline mode to mimic running downhill.

GEAR

Running is a convenient sport that can be completed almost anywhere, with minimal gear. Even so, triathlon run gear is a bit different than what you'd use for stand-alone running.

Running shoes: Since your run training is preparing you to run off the bike on race day, give careful consideration to your running shoe selection. With so many brands out there, visit your local running store to get a free gait analysis from a qualified shoe expert.

Ultimately, you want a shoe that is lightweight and responsive, but also offers structure, support, and cushioning. Because your feet swell throughout the duration of a run, leaving about ½-inch of extra space in the front of the shoe will allow your foot to move comfortably without rubbing. If you choose to run sockless on race day (which can make for a quicker bike-to-run transition), make sure the material inside your shoe is constructed with breathable fabric. This will let you run well when your feet are wet without the shoes feeling heavy and soggy, and minimizes the risk for blisters. Consider having at least two pairs of running shoes to rotate between throughout the training season. If you're tackling an off-road triathlon, you'll need trail shoes to increase traction and decrease slippage. Only wear your running shoes for running—not for everyday living. The average pair of shoes will last 300–500 miles. It's best to reinvest in a new pair every 4–6 months.

Speed laces or lace locks: This inexpensive addition to your run shoes can save you precious time by eliminating the need to tie your shoes so you can get your shoes on quickly. Remember, in a triathlon, every second counts!

Race kit: Although you may feel more comfortable running in a loose pair of running shorts and a singlet, the transition area won't offer a private place for you to change your clothes throughout the race. A one-piece triathlon suit can be worn throughout the entire race, whereas a two-piece suit (tri-top and tri-shorts) offers a less restrictive feel and is easy to remove for a quick bathroom stop. Because materials and sizes differ among brands, try out a variety of options before purchasing. Don't forget to train in your race-day kit a few times before race day (especially with swimming) so you feel comfortable and confident in your race-day outfit.

Sports bra: For women, choosing the right sports bra is essential. The wrong size or wrong type may cause breast pain and chafing. Although many tri-tops are equipped with a built-in bra, it's best to wear a sports bra for full support. You'll wear this bra throughout the entire triathlon, either as your run "top" or under your tri-kit. Practice swimming in your sports bra before race day to ensure it doesn't cause excessive drag, constriction, or chafing.

Gadgets: You can track your time with just a basic sport watch, but newer, smart watches will let you track metrics like distance, cadence, heart rate, and intervals. Most GPS running watches can be paired with a heart rate monitor, which can be worn around your arm or chest. Some watches provide an optical heart rate (no HR strap is needed), although this type of heart rate monitoring is not known to be 100 perent reliable and accurate. After your run, a Bluetooth-enabled smart watch will automatically upload your data to your preferred running app. More sophisticated watches come at a price but track additional metrics like stride length, ground contact time, vertical oscillation, and more. Select a gadget based on the features that will benefit your training, as most running watches offer more features than you actually need.

Hydration belt and race belt: To keep your hands free to comfortably swing by your sides and to reduce neck and shoulder tension, a good, ergonomically designed hydration belt (or pack) will let you carry your nutrition with you. It's sort of like having an insurance policy against dehydration, bonking (i.e., hitting the wall), and heat-related stress, by allowing you to drink on your own schedule. A race belt is a simple way to secure and wear your bib number for the duration of the run.

Running Gear Checklist

- ❏ Running shoes: $120–250
- ❏ Triathlon race kit: $100–350
- ❏ Lace locks: $3–15
- ❏ Race belt: $8–15
- ❏ Hat/visor: $25
- ❏ Hydration belt/pack: $25–70
- ❏ Sports bra (women): $25–50

SEVEN

TRANSITIONS AND BRICKS

With so much focus on improving your swim, bike, and run fitness, it's easy to neglect what happens in between each discipline on race day. Transitions are unique to triathlons, as you move from one sport to the next while making your way from start to finish. The transition area is the place where you keep your equipment and perform skills like putting on your bike helmet and running shoes. The transition area can be stressful and chaotic, but it's not an area for rest or socialization. It's important to remember that your race time includes everything that happens from the start of the swim until you reach the finish line.

Most triathletes will experience their highest race-day heart rate in the first transition area. After exiting the swim, the rush of running to your bike can make even the most experienced triathlete feel a bit winded. As with any component of triathlon, you need a plan. Well before the race, know exactly what you are going to do in the transition area and practice it. If you want a faster time on race day, consider transitions an important component of your triathlon training.

TRANSITIONS

Transitions offer a unique opportunity to save time with little physical cost. However, because real transitions are something you can only practice during a race, the transition area often contributes to physical and emotional stress on race day. Even if your training plan calls for "brick" workouts (e.g., cycling followed immediately by a run), you probably aren't transitioning with the pressure, nerves, and elevated heart rate that you will experience on race day. Because triathlon is one continuous sport, look for every possible opportunity to save time. Here are a few tips for a speedy transition:

1. **Create an auto-pilot plan.** Everything you need for the entire race will be in your designated transition area spot. You need a simple plan from swim to bike (Transition 1: T1) and bike to run (Transition 2: T2). Leaving decisions to chance costs time and increases the risk for mistakes. The less stuff you have, the less overwhelmed you will be during transition. The transition area can be crowded, so keep your space tight and orderly.

2. **Understand the transition layout.** Study the layout of the transition area. Review and rehearse your transition before every race. Look for permanent landmarks (e.g., a light post) to help you quickly locate your designated bike rack. A brightly colored transition towel/mat can also make it easy to spot your gear amidst the chaos.

3. **Understand the rules.** Every race is different, so be sure to know the specifics of your event. Some triathlons require you to put your swim and bike gear into a bag provided to you at athlete check-in. Many races don't allow personal transition bags and bike pumps to be left in the transition area throughout the race. Rules are typically explained in the athlete guide or at the pre-race athlete briefing.

4. **Visualize.** Before you finish the swim and the bike, mentally rehearse the up-coming transition process. Spend a few minutes visualizing what you need to do in the transition area. By thinking ahead, you can lessen the panic and anxiety that often occurs when it is time to finally transition.

5. **Laugh it off.** No transition will ever be flawless. Crazy things happen when you are in the race environment. The most important thing is to stay calm no matter what goes wrong. If anything, give yourself a laugh when you put your helmet on backwards or you stumble over your wobbly feet.

Transition Area Setup

Every race has a designated area called the transition area. Some races have two differ-ent transition locations, depending on the swim venue. Unless there is a last-minute change for environmental reasons, the transitioning process will be the same in every race: swim to bike (Transition 1) and bike to run (Transition 2). Except for a two-transition, point-to-point race, all of your bike and run belongings will be orga-nized on the ground in the transition area, either in front of or to the side of the front wheel of your bike.

Transition 1

As you exit the water, unzip your wetsuit or swimskin (if applicable) and pull the suit down to your waist. Some races will have volunteers (called wetsuit strippers or peelers) to help you remove your wetsuit from your body. If you are racing only in a swimsuit or tri-kit, you will skip this step. As you run, jog, or walk toward the transition

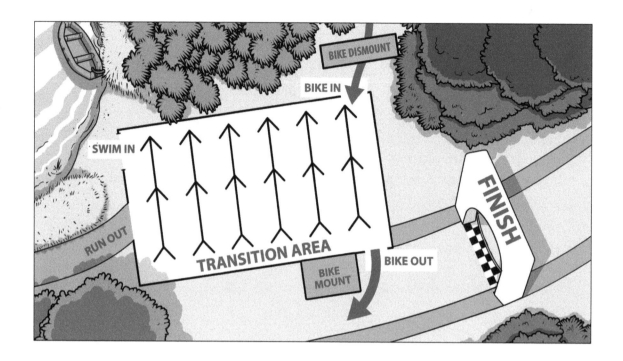

area, remove your cap and goggles. Once you reach your bike, step out of your wetsuit (if you haven't already) and place the wetsuit on the ground away from you, under the rear wheel of your bike. Put on your cycling shoes, helmet, socks (if applicable), and sunglasses, and remove your bike from the rack. Any other loose items should already be attached to your bike, as handling small items takes up precious time. To effectively run or walk with your bike, stay alongside your bike with your inside hand on the seat, pushing the bike next to or slightly in front of you. Once you reach the mount line, resist the urge to immediately mount your bike. Continue to push your bike for a few more seconds and veer away from the middle of the road. This will give you more space as you mount your bike, away from other riders. After you get on your bike, look around to make sure it's safe to start pedaling forward. Unless you are proficient at mounting your bike with your cycling shoes already attached to the pedals, put on your cycling shoes in the transition area.

After dismounting your bike before the dismount line, push your bike by the saddle to your designated rack and rack your bike in front of your belongings. You are not allowed to unbuckle your helmet until your bike is racked. Put on your running shoes (and socks, if wearing) and remove your helmet. You have the option to put on your hat or visor, sunglasses, and race belt (with bib number affixed) either at your transition spot or while walking or jogging out of transition. Don't forget your run nutrition or hydration belt. A sprinkle of baby powder or body glide around the heel of your run shoes will help your feet slide in more smoothly if you choose to run sockless.

BRICK WORKOUTS

As mentioned before, transitions count toward your total race time. Faster transitions make for a faster race time. You'll notice these workouts refer to specific zones of intensity. Please refer to pages 30–31 to see the definition of these perceived effort zones.

TRANSITION SIMULATION

Total time: 20 minutes

Fitness level: Beginner

Set up your transition area in an empty parking lot and use a floor bike stand to secure your bike. Around 20 feet away from your bike, perform 20 jumping jacks (to get your heart rate up) and then sprint to your bike. Transition to your bike gear and practice running with your bike for 20 seconds. Mount the bike, ride for a few minutes, and then dismount the bike. Now run with your bike back to your makeshift transition area before you transition to your run gear. Run for 5 minutes and continue this routine (minus the jumping jacks) for 20 minutes total. You'll notice that it becomes more difficult to complete basic tasks when your heart rate is elevated and you are tired.

As you become more experienced, practice mounting your bike with your shoes already attached to your pedals (flying mount) and then dismounting with your shoes still attached to the pedals (flying dismount).

SWIM-TO-BIKE TRANSITION

Total time: 85 minutes

Fitness level: Intermediate

You'll need your cycling shoes, a bike trainer, your bike, swimsuit, cap, and goggles. Set up your bike on your bike trainer on the deck of the pool.

Warm-up

Swim: 10 minutes easy swimming

Main set

Swim: 100 yards in Zone 1, 100 yards in Zone 2, 100 yards in Zone 3, with 10–20 seconds of rest in between. The goal is to build your effort so that the last 100-yard interval is your strongest effort. This will also help with pacing so you don't go out too hard on race day.

Follow the previous set with 200 yards (start at an easy Zone 1 effort and build to moderately strong Zone 4 effort). For this interval, you will include sighting. To practice for the open water, sight three times every lap (25 yards) throughout the 200-yard interval, while also trying to build your effort.

For less experienced swimmers, you can modify this workout by swimming 3 x 50 yards instead of 3 x 100 yards and following the set with 100 yards instead of 200 yards.

Transition: After the swim set, quickly get out of the water, remove your cap and goggles, and transition to your bike. Put on your cycling shoes and start pedaling. You do not need to wear your helmet for this workout.

Bike: 1 minute in Zone 1, 3 minutes in Zone 2, 6 minutes in Zones 3–4.

Transition: Quickly transition back to the pool and repeat this workout (starting with the main set) up to four rounds total (swim-bike-swim-bike-swim-bike-swim-bike). Make sure you are staying fueled and hydrated throughout this entire workout.

Cool down: ~10 minutes easy swimming or cycling.

BIKE-TO-RUN TRANSITION

Total time: 90 minutes

Fitness level: Experienced

You'll need your bike, cycling shoes, helmet, sunglasses, running shoes, socks (if wearing), hat/visor, and any nutrition you plan to use during the bike and run.

Warm-up

Bike: 20 minutes easy cycling

Main set

Bike: 8 minutes in Zones 3–4 followed by 4 minutes in Zone 1. Repeat two more times. This is a great set to perform in the 4–5 weeks before your race, as you begin to feel out your "race pace." Don't forget to fuel/hydrate. Finish the bike with 5 minutes in Zone 1 as you prepare your legs for the run.

Transition: To simulate race day, make sure you have your run gear set up the way you will on the day. Quickly change into your running shoes, socks, hat or visor, and sunglasses, and grab your hydration and sports nutrition. You can even practice running with your race belt, where you'll secure your bib number (which is required to be worn on your front on the run).

Run: 10 minutes in Zone 2, 5 minutes in Zones 2–3, 5 minutes in Zone 4, and 1 minute in Zone 5. Cool down with 8 minutes in Zone 1 (walk/jog). This run is another opportunity to practice pacing so that you know how to hold yourself back when running off the bike.

For a less advanced option, modify the run to: 5 minutes in Zone 2, 30-second walk, 5 minutes in Zones 2–3, 30-second walk, 3 minutes in Zone 4, 60–90 second walk, and 30 seconds in Zone 5. Cool down with 5 minutes in Zone 1 (walk/jog).

EIGHT

STRENGTH TRAINING

With every swim stroke, you need strong lats, chest muscles, abdominals, and shoulders. For cycling and running, you need strong quads, hamstrings, glutes, calves, and feet. A strong core provides better posture and support for the outer muscles and limbs. Because the efficiency behind your movements declines under fatigue, strength training can help improve economy and increase endurance. Improving the capacity of a muscle (or muscle group) to sustain activity for longer periods of time will help you go farther, faster.

Although trying to squeeze another activity into your already-packed schedule may look impossible, you can make yourself a better triathlete with no more than 90 minutes of strength training per week. That comes out to no more than 30 minutes, just 3 times per week! Even the most basic at-home full-body strength training program will increase the strength of your muscles, bones, tendons, and ligaments. When muscle imbalances are fixed and tissues are strengthened, you can place more load on them, which means better training and less risk of an injury-related setback.

DYNAMIC WARM-UP

A dynamic warm-up is designed to gradually increase your heart rate and blood flow, to awaken the muscles, and to excite the nervous system. Actively moving your body will also increase range of motion while getting your mind into a workout-ready state.

Bench Taps

Targets: glutes, quadriceps, hamstrings, soleus, gastrocnemius, hip flexors, abdominals

1. Stand in front of a box or step 10–15 inches high.
2. Tap your left toe on the step, and then quickly switch sides, landing softly with bent knees.
3. Continue, alternating legs, tapping your toes quickly yet with control in a running-like manner.
4. Perform the exercise for 20–30 seconds, then rest before repeating.

Tip: Instead of a box or step, you can use a medicine ball or simply tap the floor.

Butt Kicks

Targets: hamstrings, quadriceps, glutes, hip flexors

1. Stand tall with your feet shoulder-width apart and arms bent by your sides.
2. Bend your left knee, kicking your left foot back and up toward your glutes.
3. As you return your left foot to the ground, simultaneously flex your right knee and kick your right foot back toward your glutes.
4. Continue switching sides, allowing your arms to swing back and forth as though you were jogging, keeping your knees slightly bent.
5. Gradually increase speed as you build confidence. The faster you move, the more you will work your fast-twitch muscle fibers.
6. Perform sets of 10–20 seconds in duration, resting between sets.

Tip: When you bring your heel up, don't swing it to the side. Make sure your heel goes straight to your glute. When you begin to speed up the move, you are likely to get sloppy. Start slowly as the movement requires coordination.

Power Skips

Targets: hamstrings, quadriceps, abdominals, glutes, hip flexors, calves

1. Stand tall with your feet hip-width apart, with arms raised to waist height.
2. Forcefully drive through your feet, to elevate your left knee and explosively lift yourself into the air as high as possible. Raise your right hand up in the air and allow your left hand to swing backward.
3. Land on the balls of your feet and then immediately drive through your feet again, this time elevating your right knee.
4. Continue alternating sides in a rhythmic manner until you have completed 10–15 skips on each side.

Tip: If you are warming up or suffer any knee problems, keep your knees low and slightly slow down the movement.

Fire Hydrants

Targets: glutes, hip flexors, abdominals

1. Start by kneeling on all fours with your hands directly beneath your shoulders and knees beneath your hips.
2. Lift your right leg away from your body at a 45-degree angle. Maintain a 90-degree angle through your knee and keep your back straight.
3. Return your leg to the starting position.
4. Complete repetitions on one side and then repeat with the other leg.

Tip: Don't rock or tilt your hips. It's important to open your hip during this move, rather than elevating your knee, dropping your hip, or rotating your chest.

Skaters

Targets: hamstrings, quadriceps, glutes, abdominals, calves

1. Stand with your feet shoulder-width apart, with knees slightly bent. Brace your core and lean forward slightly while keeping your back straight.
2. Jump laterally to the left, landing on your left foot while bending your knee to absorb the impact. Simultaneously bring your right arm in front of you.
3. Switch sides, jumping laterally to the right, this time bringing your left leg behind you and your left arm forwards.
4. Keep alternating back and forth for 20–30 seconds. Rest, and then start another set.

Tip: This exercise is a great run warm-up for the lower body muscles and to help with ankle stabilization. To prevent your knee and ankle from collapsing inward, maintain tight pelvic control and glute strength.

Step-up with Knee Raise

Targets: quadriceps, hamstrings, hip flexors, abdominals, calves

1. Stand in front of a box or step, 15–20 inches high, with your feet together.
2. Place your left foot on the box and then, while bracing your core, extend through your left hip and knee to stand tall on the box while raising your right knee high in the air until your right thigh is parallel to the floor.
3. Reverse this motion and step down carefully, placing your right foot back on the ground.
4. Alternate sides, stepping on the right foot to raise your left knee.
5. Continue alternating sides, until you have completed 10 repetitions on each side. Complete three sets per side.

Tip: Once you have mastered this exercise using your own body weight, hold dumbbells for an added challenge. Keep your hips neutral and maintain control (to prevent wobbling) by engaging your glutes.

LOWER BODY

To give you power when you cycle and propulsion when you run, the following exercises will help you build strength and endurance in your hips, glutes, quads, hamstrings, calves, and feet.

Lunge to Pause

Targets: quadriceps, calves, glutes, hip flexors, abdominals, lower back

1. Stand with your feet hip-width apart, with your hands on your hips. Hold a tight core without arching your back.
2. Step your left foot back behind your left hip and bend your right knee to a 90-degree angle, until your left knee rests slightly above the floor. Ensure your right knee remains in line with your right ankle. Hold this position for one second.
3. Brace your core and drive through your right heel, extending your hips back to the starting position.
4. After you finish a set, switch sides.

Tip: Knee pain can result if your glutes are not doing their job or if your form is poor. You can modify this exercise by shortening your stride length or only going one-fourth of the way down.

Wall Sit

Targets: glutes, hamstrings, hip flexors, quadriceps, calves, abdominals

1. Stand with your back against a wall, then walk your feet forward 6–12 inches, keeping them shoulder-width apart.
2. Engage your abdominal muscles and slowly slide down the wall until your thighs are parallel to the ground and knees are bent at 90 degrees. You should feel like you are sitting in a chair. You may have to walk your feet out a few inches to make sure your weight is in your heels and your knees are over your ankles rather than your toes.
3. Hold this position for 20, 30, or 60 seconds, keeping your back flat against the wall throughout. Then, slide slowly back up the wall to return to a standing position before repeating.

Tip: If this exercise places pressure on your lower back or knees, place an exercise ball between your back and the wall to make it more comfortable. If you are feeling strain in your knees and not in your glutes, slightly turn your knees outward.

Bridge

Targets: glutes, hip flexors, hamstrings, abdominals, lower back

1. Lie faceup on the floor with your knees bent, feet flat and hip-width apart, and arms extended by your sides.
2. Engage your core by tilting your pelvis toward your belly button and slowly lift your hips off the floor, forming a diagonal line from your knees to your shoulders, keeping your head, shoulders, and arms down.
3. Hold for three seconds, contracting your glutes and pressing your heels into the floor, and then lower to the starting position.

Tip: Be careful not to hyperextend your lower back by pushing your hips too high. Perform this exercise slowly.

Kettlebell Squats

Targets: glutes, hip flexors, hamstrings, quadriceps, abdominals, lower back, triceps

1. Stand tall with your feet slightly wider than shoulder-width apart, toes pointed slightly outward.
2. Using both hands, hold a kettlebell with an overhand grip at chest level.
3. Brace your core and bend your knees, lowering your hips until your thighs are parallel with the floor. Keep your chest high, back straight, and elbows tucked by your sides throughout the movement.
4. Drive through your heels to push back up to the starting position, contracting your glutes hard at the top.

Tip: Make sure your knees are not going too far past your toes as you squat down. Because your heels are a driving force of the upward move, make sure your heels don't come off the ground. To engage the glutes, keep your knees slightly outward (not inward).

Single Leg Glute Bridge

Targets: glutes, hip flexors, abdominals, hamstrings, quadriceps

1. Lie faceup on the floor with your knees bent and feet flat on the floor. Hold a kettlebell at your chest with both hands.
2. Lift your hips off the floor until you are in a fully extended glute bridge position. Using your left hand, transfer the kettlebell to rest on your left bicep. Lift your right leg keeping your hips neutral and glutes tight.
3. Squeeze your chest and push the kettlebell directly up toward the ceiling, pushing your shoulder blade into the ground and keeping your elbow tucked closely into your torso. Hold this position for 3-5 seconds. Then slowly lower your hips to the starting position while continuing to hold up the kettlebell.
4. Slowly lower the kettlebell and repeat on the opposite side.

Tip: Don't let your hips drop while holding the glute bridge position.

Calf Raises

Targets: calves

1. Stand on a raised step, with your feet hip-width apart. The balls of your feet should be firmly positioned on the step, with your heels slightly hanging off. Keep your hands by your sides or hold on to a wall for balance.
2. Slowly raise yourself to stand tall on the balls of your feet, extending your ankles as high as possible.
3. Hold for one second and then slowly lower yourself back down to the starting position, feeling a stretch through your calf muscles.

Tip: To help with Achilles issues, try eccentric calf raises. Start on your tiptoes on a step and slowly lower your heel below the forefoot. Use the other leg to raise yourself back to the starting position.

CORE/BACK

A strong core is essential for maintaining good stability and posture in the later miles of a run, especially when running off the bike. As you strengthen your core muscles, your swimming, biking, and running form and efficiency should improve, helping you become more resistant to fatigue.

Forearm Plank

Targets: abdominals

1. Lie facedown on the floor, with your legs extended behind you and feet hip-width apart. Your elbows should be bent and aligned beneath your shoulders, and your forearms and palms should be flat on the floor.
2. Engage your abs by pulling your pelvis toward your belly button and tuck your toes to lift your hips off the floor, forming a straight line from your head to your heels. Be careful not to raise or drop your hips, and keep your neck in a neutral position by looking at the floor about a foot in front of your hands.
3. Hold this position for up to 60 seconds, then lower to the starting position before repeating

Tip: To make this exercise easier, you can do a straight arm plank with your palms on the floor (instead of resting your elbows on the floor). For added difficulty, rotate from side, front, to side by holding each move for 15–30 seconds. You can also alternate lifting one arm and the opposite leg.

Mountain Climbers

Targets: abdominals, glutes, hip flexors, chest, shoulders

1. Start in a straight-arm plank position with your palms on the floor under your shoulders and your legs extended behind you. Keep your back flat, your abs engaged, and your toes tucked under.
2. Bring your left knee toward your chest using your core (not your lower back), keeping your right leg straight.
3. Keeping your hands on the ground, abs tight, shoulders down, and body low to the ground, hop to switch legs so your right knee is forward and left leg is back. Keep your body in a straight line and do not let your head drop.
4. Continue alternating sides quickly but efficiently—similar to mirroring a running motion.
5. Continue for up to 30 seconds, rest, and repeat.

Tip: For an added challenge, you can do this exercise by starting with your legs on a stability ball (instead of the floor). You can also perform this exercise by bringing your left knee to the right shoulder and vice versa.

Exercise Bicycle

Targets: abdominals, obliques, glutes, hip flexors

1. Lie faceup on the floor with your feet off the floor, with your knees bent over your hips. Interlace your fingers behind your head, with elbows pointing out to your sides. Press your lower back into the ground.
2. Keeping your right knee bent, extend your left leg down toward the floor as you lift your upper body off the floor and rotate your torso to your right, bringing your left elbow to your right knee.
3. Rotate your torso back through the center to your legs; switch sides, bringing your right elbow to your left knee.
4. Continue alternating, as if you were pedaling a bike. Don't rush this exercise or make it sloppy.

Tip: For a more advanced version, the elevated bicycle crunch can be performed while sitting on a bench. Since your legs drop lower to the ground, your core has to work harder to lift them as you twist. This modification can become more challenging with added weight as you rotate side to side.

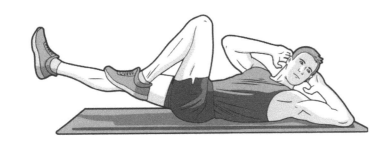

Alternating Heel Touches

Targets: abdominals, obliques

1. Lie faceup on the floor with your knees bent, feet flat on the floor, and arms extended by your sides. Keep your back flat on the floor.
2. Raise your shoulders slightly to crunch your torso and reach toward the right, touching your right heel with your right hand. Hold for one second.
3. Return to the starting position and then repeat on the left side.
4. Keep alternating.

Tip: A similar exercise would be a standing side crunch where you hold a weight and bend to the opposite side.

Superman

Targets: lower and upper back, abdominals, shoulders

1. Lie facedown on the floor, with your arms extended overhead and your legs extended behind you.
2. Engage your core and keep your shoulders down as you simultaneously lift your arms, chest, and legs several inches off the ground. Your body should form an elongated U-shape.
3. Hold this position for one breath, squeezing your lower back and keeping your neck in a neutral position, and then gently lower back down to the starting position.

Tip: To modify this exercise, you can alternate lifting your right arm and your left leg, holding and then switching. For more difficulty, you can perform this exercise on a stability ball by lifting only your legs and keeping your hands on the ground in front of you.

UPPER BODY

A strong upper body is needed for more than just swimming. Cycling requires a strong upper body for handling the bike, especially when climbing. While running, your arms help save energy by driving you forward with each foot strike.

One Arm Kettlebell Press

Targets: shoulders, triceps, biceps, abdominals, glutes, hip flexors, quadriceps, calves, hamstrings

1. Hold a kettlebell in your right hand. Lift it toward your right shoulder, rotating your wrist so your palm faces forward.
2. Bend your knees slightly and, without pausing, push the kettlebell overhead as you straighten your legs.
3. Reverse the movement by lowering the weight to your right shoulder to return to the starting position.
4. Complete repetitions on the right side and then switch to the left side.

Tip: Your legs and arm should be extended in the overhead position, but not locked or hyperextended. Keep your torso upright throughout the movement.

Alternating Plank Row

Targets: upper and lower back, abdominals, triceps, biceps, chest, traps

1. Begin in a full-arm plank position, with palms on the ground.
2. Brace your core and bend your left elbow, drawing your hand up to the left side of your body and squeezing your shoulder blades together. Keep your body in a straight line, squeezing your glutes and core. Resist your body's natural inclination to twist upward by engaging your obliques.
3. Hold for one count before returning your hand to the floor.
4. Repeat on the right side before resting and repeating the exercise.

Tip: Once you have mastered this exercise, hold dumbbells to make this move more challenging.

Bent Over Barbell Row

Targets: biceps, upper, middle and lower back, lats, traps

1. Set up a barbell with the appropriate amount of weight on the floor in front of you. Bend your knees slightly and, holding the barbell with a wide overhand grip, lift it from the floor carefully, keeping your back, head, and neck straight.
2. While exhaling, slowly pull the barbell toward your upper stomach, feeling the contraction in your lats. Keep your torso at a 45-degree angle, with your elbows close to your sides.
3. While inhaling, lower the weight until your arms are extended and shoulders are gently stretched downward.

Tip: You can also perform this exercise with free weights instead of a barbell.

Single Arm Glute Bridge Press

Targets: chest, shoulders, biceps, triceps, abdominals, glutes, hip flexors

1. Lie faceup on the floor with your knees bent and feet flat on the floor. Hold a kettlebell at your chest with both hands.
2. Lift your hips off the floor until you are in a fully extended glute bridge position. Using your left hand, transfer the kettlebell to rest on your left bicep.
3. Squeeze your chest and push the kettlebell directly up toward the ceiling, pushing your shoulder blade into the ground and keeping your elbow tucked closely into your torso.
4. Slowly lower the kettlebell and complete your desired repetitions on your left side, and then repeat on the right side, holding the kettlebell with your right hand.

Tip: Although much of your focus will be on what your arm is doing, don't let your hips drop while holding the glute bridge position.

NINE

STRETCHING

For a muscle to have the capability to deliver full power and strength, it must have good range of motion. For example, if your hip flexors get tight from repetitive cycling or prolonged periods of sitting in the car, you won't be able to extend to a full stride while running and you may experience back pain when riding your bike. Stretching can't prevent an injury, but it may help reduce the risk of one occurring in the first place. Because triathlon lacks lateral or side-to-side movement, mobility exercises can improve the many imbalances that can result from constantly exercising in a single forward plane of motion.

STRETCHES

Mobility exercises can be performed any time of the day. But when performing mobility exercises around a workout, it's always better to stretch a warm muscle after a warm-up activity like jogging or walking. Unlike static stretching—holding a muscle in a stretched position—dynamic stretching and mobility exercises are recommended as part of your warm-up routine. The goal of stretching is to become more mobile—not more flexible. Mobility can help improve movement patterns and range of motion. You can also incorporate these mobility exercises into your daily routine (e.g., during your lunch break).

Calf Stretch

Targets: calf, feet

1. Sit up straight on the floor or mat. Bend both knees with your heels on the floor.
2. Take a rope and hold the ends together so that it forms a loop. Place the foot of the leg you're stretching into the loop. Stretch that leg out into a straight position.
3. Grasp the end of the rope with both hands (to maintain the loop).
4. Activate the shin muscle on the front of your leg; this will cause your toes to come toward your body and pull slightly with the rope. Hold this stretch for 2–3 seconds and relax; repeat several times. Switch legs.

Tip: Bands are great for loosening up really tight calves. It's suggested to lightly foam roll your calves before performing this stretch.

Bent-Knee Hamstring

Targets: hamstrings, calves

1. Lie on your back. Begin with one knee bent and foot flat on the floor, and bring the other knee close to your chest.
2. Take a rope and hold the ends together so that it forms a loop. Place the foot of the leg you're stretching into the loop. Lift your leg until your thigh is perpendicular to the floor.
3. Grasp the end of the rope with two hands (to maintain the loop). Gradually extend your leg by contracting your quadriceps. This will cause your foot to rise toward the ceiling. Stop the stretch when you feel a slight tug in the back of your leg. Point your toes toward you for a deeper stretch.

Tip: To feel the full stretch, you may need to lower the angle of your leg from the hip at first. Use the rope for gentle assistance at the end of the stretch. Do not forcefully pull your leg into position.

Shoulder Rotations

Targets: shoulders

1. Stand with your feet about shoulder-width apart, toes slightly turned out, and knees softly bent.
2. Extend your arms out to your sides so your body forms a T-shape. Keep the natural arch in your lower back and your chin parallel to the floor.
3. With palms facing forward, bend your arms until your elbows form 90-degree angles.
4. Contract your core muscles and quickly lower your palms until they're parallel with the floor.
5. Reverse direction and repeat the forearm movements.

Tip: Keep your triceps and chin parallel to the floor at all times. You can also move your arms into a T, then a W, and then a V for additional stretches.

Quad Stretch

Targets: quadriceps

1. Stand next to a wall for support. Place one hand on the wall. Tuck in your pelvis to prevent an exaggerated anterior pelvic tilt. Hold this pelvic position as you raise your opposing ankle up with the free hand.

2. Hold this stretch for 2–3 seconds while continually contracting your hamstring and glutes on the side you are stretching.

3. Lower your foot down to the ground and repeat.

Tip: Be sure to keep your back straight and pelvis tucked inward (don't arch your back). Arching your back decreases the amount of stretch in the muscle.

Myofascial Release

Targets: back, neck, calves, feet, quads, hamstrings

1. Sit on the ground and place a foam roller under a specific muscle group to reduce tightness and soreness or to increase blood flow.
2. Slowly position your body so the specific muscle group that you want to target (e.g., calves, quads) ends up on top of the foam roller.
3. Move your body back and forth on the foam roller, using small (2- to 6-inch) continuous movements, applying gentle pressure to any tender areas where you feel discomfort.

Tip: If you have a particularly sore and tender spot, apply pressure near, but not directly over, the area. You should never feel pain on any tender area you are targeting. If you do, release some pressure.

Bird Dog

Targets: hip flexors, upper back, abdominals, lower back

1. Begin in a hands-and-knees position with your wrists aligned beneath your shoulders and knees beneath your hips; your fingers should point forward.
2. Tuck your right toes under and extend your right leg behind you. Slowly lift your leg off the floor, raising it no higher than hip height.
3. Brace your core gently so you maintain an elongated spine. Slowly reach your left arm forward, no higher than shoulder height, and turn your palm to face inward while pointing your thumb toward the ceiling. Hold this extended position for 5–6 seconds, keeping your hips and shoulders level.
4. Return to the starting position and repeat the movement on your opposite side.

Tip: When this exercise becomes easier for you, increase the number of repetitions you do, instead of holding your arm and leg for a longer period of time. Avoid shifting your weight when alternating sides. Keep your body weight centered.

Ankle Circles

Targets: ankles, feet

1. Sit near the edge of a chair with both feet firmly planted on the floor and your hands resting on your thighs.
2. Lift your right foot off the floor and extend your right leg slightly away from your body.
3. Without moving your lifted leg, rotate your foot clockwise at the ankle. Complete this movement, then repeat it going counterclockwise.
4. Repeat with the left foot.

Tip: An alternative to this exercise is writing the letters of the alphabet, from A to Z, with one foot at a time.

Cat Cow

Targets: neck, shoulders, spine, hip flexors, chest

1. Begin in a hands-and-knees position, with your wrists aligned beneath your shoulders and your knees aligned beneath your hips. Keep your spine extended and your toes tucked under.
2. Inhale, relax your belly so it moves toward the floor, and gently arch your back, tilting your tailbone and chin toward the ceiling.
3. Exhale, gently round your spine, draw your chin toward your chest, and untuck your toes, placing the tops of your feet on the floor.
4. Repeat this sequence of movements.

Tip: Don't rush this exercise. Focus on your breathing and posture throughout the entire cat-cow movement process. Think about the movement of your lower abs and pelvis to take the pressure off your lower back.

Quad Rotations

Targets: abdominals, back, shoulders, chest

1. Begin in a hands-and-knees position with your knees aligned beneath your hips and your wrists beneath your shoulders.
2. Draw your left fingertips behind your left ear, keeping your elbow bent and open to the side of your body.
3. Rotate your torso to your left, drawing your left elbow to point toward the ceiling.
4. Reverse the movement, returning your torso to your starting position parallel with the floor while crossing your left elbow toward your right arm. Continue this movement.
5. Switch sides and repeat.

Tip: If your wrists or knees bother you when you are in a hands-and-knees position, try this dynamic stretch while seated, with both sets of fingers behind your ears and your elbows out wide.

Downward-Facing Dog

Targets: hip flexors, hamstrings, calves, ankles, arms, shoulders

1. Begin on your hands and knees, with your knees aligned below your hips and your hands slightly in front of your shoulders, fingers spread wide.
2. Press your palms firmly into the floor. Inhale while tucking your toes under.
3. Exhale while you extend your legs, lifting your hips and tailbone toward the ceiling to create an inverted V-shape with your body, drawing your heels toward the floor while you maintain length in your spine. Hold this stretch.

Tip: To ensure proper form for this yoga-inspired pose, engage your upper arms and allow your head and neck to remain positioned between your biceps as you hold this stretch. As you push your thighs back and lift the sit bones toward the ceiling, stretch your heels down toward the floor without locking your knees.

Half Lord of the Fishes

Targets: chest, shoulders, hip flexors, back, neck

1. Sit on the floor with your legs stretched out in front of you. Bend your right knee and step your right foot over your left thigh, planting your right foot on the floor outside your left knee.
2. Place your right hand on the floor behind your right hip with your fingers pointed away from your body. Inhale and lift your left arm toward the ceiling while lengthening your spine.
3. Exhale, gently rotate your torso to the right, hugging your right knee with your left arm or hooking your left elbow outside your right knee. Gaze over your right shoulder, if you can manage it. Hold this stretch.
4. Switch sides and repeat.

Tip: For more support and comfort, sit on a folded blanket, towel, or foam block. For a more intense stretch, bend your extended leg, folding your heel in toward your opposite glute. Maintain length in your spine when performing this stretch and allow your head to turn to face the same direction you are twisting.

Open Heart Stretch

Targets: chest, shoulders, neck, upper back

1. While seated, interlace your hands behind the upper back of your head, close to the crown.
2. Gently pull your head forward, guiding your chin toward your chest while keeping your elbows open as wide as possible. Hold this stretch.

Tip: To get the most out of this stretch, avoid rounding your shoulders forward. Instead, focus on engaging the muscles between your shoulder blades to keep your shoulders pulled back and your elbows open wide.

Leg Swings

Target: hip flexors

1. Stand with your feet slightly parted and your hands resting on your hips.
2. Shift your weight to your left foot, bending your right knee slightly while lifting your right heel.
3. Keeping your right knee softly bent, actively swing your right leg forward and backward, allowing your right knee to naturally bend and extend throughout the movement, all while keeping your back straight. Continue this movement.
4. Switch sides and repeat.

Tip: Your torso should remain stable during this exercise. This is an excellent exercise to perform before running or cycling.

Thread the Needle

Targets: shoulders, back, neck, chest, arms

1. From a hands-and-knees position, turn your head to the left and slide your right arm along the floor underneath your left arm, positioning your palm to face the ceiling.
2. Keep your hips stacked over your knees, extend your left arm fully in front of your body, and press your right forearm and upper arm (if possible) firmly into the floor. Hold this stretch.
3. Switch sides and repeat.

Tip: Keep your forearm pressed firmly into the floor and use the ground as leverage when performing this stretch.

Supine Spinal Twist

Targets: back, hip flexors

1. While lying on your back with your knees bent and feet flat, stretch your left leg along the floor, keeping a slight bend in the knee.
2. Inhale, lift your right foot, and, with your hands, draw your right knee toward your chest.
3. Exhale, extend your right arm, palm facing up, out to your right side. With your left hand, gently guide your right knee across your body to fall outside your left hip.
4. Turn your head to look toward your right hand. Hold this stretch.
5. Switch sides and repeat.

Tip: For more support, place a foam block on the outside of your hip and rest your bent knee on top of the block. To vary the sensation, scoot your hips slightly toward the direction of your outstretched arm and use your other hand as leverage on your bent knee to deepen the rotation and stretch.

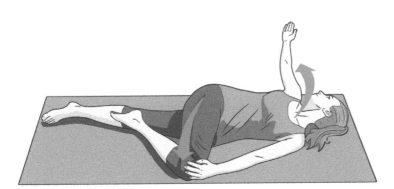

TEN

THE 12-WEEK TRAINING PLANS

This is what you have been waiting for! In this chapter, all of the training components that have been explained so far are pulled together in one easy-to-follow 12-week training plan. As you make the transition from single-sport to multisport athlete, the first and most important step in your development is establishing a solid foundation before progressing to more race-specific training.

Although you may have great experience and fitness in one sport, adapting to new training stressors (and a new sport altogether) requires patience. Rush the process or skip steps and your risk of injury increases—or you may consistently underperform. For the time-crunched athlete, the bike and run workouts are prescribed by time, rather than distance. The swim workouts, which present the biggest time variable for every athlete, are prescribed by yards. Strength training and mobility/stretching can be performed before and/or after a workout or as a separate workout for the day. The workout order for each day is a suggestion, but you are welcome to adjust based on your schedule.

NOTE FOR SWIMMERS

Not only do you have a physical and mental advantage in the first stage of the triathlon, you've also spent years building your aerobic engine, which will give you a solid base for cycling and running. Although you've taught yourself how to efficiently hold and move yourself through the water, your lower body muscles may be lacking the strength, coordination, and power needed for running and cycling. With exceptional endurance, you may feel like you can handle more bike and run volume, but more is not necessarily better. Because open water swimming is very different than the controlled environment of swimming in the pool, you may need to slightly alter your stroke to adapt to the unpredictable nature of triathlon swimming. So long as you can maintain consistency with your cycling, running, and strength training—and you have the available time and energy—you are welcome to increase swim volume for each assigned swim workout, based on your current swim fitness level.

NOTE FOR CYCLISTS

Since the bike portion makes up most of the volume of a triathlon event, your experience gives you a competitive edge over the rest of the field. From mental strength, power, and superior bike-handling skills, you'll likely find yourself advancing within the first few miles of the bike. However, if you don't dedicate proper training time to swimming, your cycling advantage can easily disappear. One of the biggest mistakes in a triathlon is going too hard on the bike and taxing your running legs. Proper bike pacing will allow you to put together a strong run off the bike—making for a better all-around triathlon experience. There's no fun in bragging about being an uber-biker if you can't run well off the bike. Due to your experience and fitness on the bike, if you have the available time and energy, you are welcome to increase cycling volume to each assigned bike workout, based on your current cycling fitness level—so long as you don't neglect your swim and run training.

NOTE FOR RUNNERS

Although you may be a strong runner, running off the bike is very different than stand-alone running. It may feel unnatural and uncomfortable. Don't be surprised if your normal gait is reduced to a shuffle (or walk) during your first few bike-to-run workouts. Due to the redirection of blood from your quads (major cycling muscle groups) to hamstrings and calves (muscles more directly involved in running), your legs may feel extremely heavy and unstable when you run off the bike. Learning how to work through this discomfort requires time and training. With the right run training, nutrition strategy, and swim and bike fitness, finding your land legs will become progressively easier. Instead of practicing each sport separately, you'll notice several different types of brick workouts in your training plan to help you prepare for the unique demands of race day. You may feel like you can or should do more run volume or intensity, but it's best to complete the training plan as written to ensure that you are triathlon fit—not just run fit.

TRAINING ZONES

The training plans in this chapter use RPE (ratings of perceived exertion) as your primary metric. Although it's fine to use power and heart rate training zones, RPE is a valuable training tool that is free, reliable, and easy to use. As you become more experienced, you will become better at associating RPE with your other metrics—if you choose to use a power meter, pace watch, and/or heart rate monitor. As a triathlete, it's important to know how to listen to your body when it comes to pacing and workout execution.

Z1 (RPE 4/10): Easy

This is an easily sustainable effort. It should feel ridiculously easy to hold good form. You can't go too easy, so be sure to enjoy it.

Z2 (RPE 5/10): Smooth

Not as easy as Z1, this is a comfortable level of effort—one that you can maintain for several hours. You should be able to hold a conversation (full sentences) for the entire length of the workout.

Z3 (RPE 6–7/10): Steady

You can sustain this effort for a reasonable amount of time, but it's sure to make you experience some fatigue and soreness. You shouldn't feel breathless, but conversation is limited to simple and quick responses. Because you will feel like you are getting in a great workout in this zone, many athletes fall into the trap of training in this zone for every workout. Why is it a trap? Because it's not easy enough to experience true aerobic benefits, and it's not hard enough to produce lactic acid from anaerobic glycolysis (breaking down glucose for energy).

Z4 (RPE 8–9/10): Strong

This zone is uncomfortable. Breathing is labored and you can barely speak. It requires great focus to hold an effort. Because of its intensity, this effort is usually reserved for high intensity intervals of short duration. Go too hard in this zone for too long and you will experience great fatigue and increase your risk for injury.

Z5 (RPE 10/10): Very Strong

This effort is extremely uncomfortable and is limited to very short efforts. It's nearly impossible to speak a word at this effort. Because intervals at this effort are so short, it's likely that your mind will want to quit before your body does.

READING THE TRAINING PLANS

In the interest of brevity, the following training plans are written in a kind of code—a shorthand for triathletes, if you will. Here's everything you need to know to help you better understand the insider lingo in your triathlon training plan.

Color Coding

Orange: Warm-up

Blue: Main set

Green: Cool down

Abbreviations

Btw: Between

B: Pull buoy

S: Snorkel

A: Ankle strap/lock

F: Fins

P: Paddles

RPM: Revolutions per minute

25 = 1 lap of pool (from wall to wall, no turn included)

Note: Although not specified, all swim sets should be freestyle. You are welcome to incorporate other strokes (breaststroke or backstroke), especially during warm-up or post-set. If you are unable to complete a workout as planned, scale the workout to your fitness ability and time constraints while still maintaining the structure of the workout.

Definitions

Ankle strap/lock: This tool binds your feet together to eliminate the use of your legs for kicking and therefore puts your body in a tighter position. Helps to minimize excessive hip rotation and drag. Most triathletes will need to use a pull buoy with the ankle strap to start for an added lift of the legs.

Brick: Immediately going from one sport to another (e.g., swim and then bike, bike and then run, swim and then run).

Drills: A movement that is designed to improve coordination, speed, agility, power, strength, or technique.

Fins: An extension of your feet, helping to improve ankle flexibility, propulsion, fluency, and movement through the water. Fins are not used to kick harder or to go faster. An intermediate blade length is advised.

High and low cadence/gear: Variable cadence drills recruit different muscle fibers and improve neurological motor patterns during the pedal stroke for more efficient pedaling.

Mobility/stretching: Dedicate 10–20 minutes to the body parts that are most sore/tight/weak. It's also advised to perform before workouts as part of an active warm-up.

Power walk: On the treadmill, incline should be 12–15%. Do not hold the treadmill. Instead, use your arms as you would in outdoor running. Stand upright and activate the glutes and posterior chain (back-of-the-leg muscles). This is a way to build strength as a triathlon runner.

Pull buoy: Placed between the upper thighs, this tool provides a base of support to lift the lower half of the body. Use this tool to learn how to sustain a better body position and to minimize the use of the legs to emphasize upper body power and strength.

Sighting: Lifting the head so the eyes are out of the water as you look for an object to keep you on course.

Single leg drill: To improve pedaling efficiency. Pedal smoothly with only one leg. Let the other leg hang down, unclipped from the pedal (don't rest it on anything). Focus on even chain tension to avoid feeling a "click" on the top of your stroke (which demonstrates a dead spot in your pedal stroke). Adjust gears as needed.

Small paddles: This tool provides a strength component to swimming. Certain paddle designs can help promote a better catch while reinforcing proper elbow and forearm position underwater. The proper paddle should be slightly bigger than your hand.

Snorkel: This tool eliminates the need to move your head to take a breath. This tool is helpful when you want to focus on technique, especially during drill sets. A nose clip may be needed if you are getting water in your nose.

Strength: Dedicate 20–30 minutes, any time of the day or around cardio sessions. Select several exercises from each body group and perform 2–3 sets of 8–12 reps. Moderate to heavy weight is advised at least once a week.

Strides: Gradually accelerate your running stride from easy to strong, while keeping a fast leg turnover.

SPRINT DISTANCE

WEEK 1	MONDAY	TUESDAY	WEDNESDAY
	1100 YARD SWIM	**30 MIN BIKE**	**1300 YARD SWIM**
	200 Z1	10 min Z1	Rest 10 sec btw:
	Use S/B/A, Z1, rest 10 sec btw:	5 x (30 sec Z2 at 90+ rpm, 90 sec Z1 at choice cadence)	200 Z1
	4 x 25		Use F: 200 Z1 kick
	2 x 50	10 min Z1	8 x 25 (odds Z4, evens Z1)
	2 x 75	**20 MIN RUN (brick or second workout)**	Use S/B/A: 3 x (150 Z2, 50 Z3, rest 20 sec btw)
	2 x 50		100 Z1
	4 x 25	5 min walk	**Strength**
	Rest 10-20 sec btw:	10 min Z1 run	
	100 Z2	5 min walk	
	50 Z3	**Mobility/stretching**	
	4 x 25 Z4		
	100 Z1		
	Strength		

THURSDAY	FRIDAY	SATURDAY	SUNDAY
40 MIN BIKE	Mobility/stretching	**800 YARD SWIM**	**36 MIN RUN**

40 MIN BIKE

20 min build Z1 to Z2

3 min Z2 at 45–55 rpm
1 min Z1 at 90+ rpm
3 min Z2 at 55–65 rpm
3 min Z1 at choice cadence

10 min Z1

12 MIN RUN (brick)

2 min walk

3 min Z1 run
1 min walk
3 min Z1 run
1 min walk

2 min walk

Mobility/stretching

FRIDAY

Mobility/stretching

800 YARD SWIM

200 Z1
Use B/A: 6 x 25 Z4, rest 10 sec btw
50 Z1

3 x 100 Z3, rest 10 sec btw

100 Z1

60 MIN BIKE (brick or second workout)

If outside: Work on bike handling skills and changing gears.
If inside: Keep at Z1-Z2 effort.

Mobility/stretching

36 MIN RUN

5 min walk
5 min Z1 run
1 min walk

4 x (4 min Z2 run, 1 min walk)

5 min Z1 run or walk

Mobility/stretching

WEEK 2

MONDAY	TUESDAY	WEDNESDAY
1450 YARD SWIM	**40 MIN BIKE**	**1300 YARD SWIM**
200 Z1	15 min Z1	Rest 20 sec btw:
Use S/B/A, Z2, rest 15 sec btw:	5 x (30 sec Z2 at 90+ rpm, 90 sec Z1 at choice cadence)	200 Z1
100	15 min Z1	Use S/B: 200
75	**20 MIN RUN (brick or second workout)**	Use F: 100 kick Z1
50	3 min walk	Use S/B/A:
25	15 min Z1 run w/ 20–30 sec walk every 5 min	3 x 100 Z2, rest 15 sec btw
25	2 min walk	9 x 50 build in sets of 3 (Z2, Z3, Z4 by 50), rest 15 sec btw
50	**Mobility/stretching**	50 Z1
75		**Strength**
100		
Rest 15 sec btw:		
Use B: 200 Z2		
Use B: 2 x 100 (75 Z2, 25 Z4)		
3 x 50 (25 Z2, 25 Z4) w/ 10–15 sec rests		
50 Z1		
4 x 25 (odds build to fast, evens easy to fast), rest 10 sec btw		
50 Z1		
Strength		

THURSDAY	FRIDAY	SATURDAY	SUNDAY
45 MIN BIKE	**Strength**	**900 YARD SWIM**	**40 MIN RUN**
15 min build Z1 to Z2		200 Z1 Use B/A: 8 x 25 Z5, rest 5 sec btw	6 min walk 3 min Z1 run 1 min walk 3 min Z1 run 1 min walk
4 min Z2, 45-55 rpm 1 min Z1, 90+ rpm 4 min Z2, 55-65 rpm 1 min Z1, 90+ rpm Repeat 1 more time		3 x 100 Z3, rest 20 sec btw	
		3 x 50 Z3, rest 10 sec btw	4 x (4 min Z2, 1 min walk)
10 min Z1		50 Z1	6 min Z1
15 MIN RUN **(brick)**		**65 MIN BIKE** **(brick)**	**Mobility/stretching**
3 min walk		20 min Z1	
4 min Z1 run 30 sec walk 4 min Z2 run 30 sec walk 3 min walk		10 x 30 sec single leg drills (alternate each leg 4 times) 10 min Z1 Repeat 1 more time 15 min Z1	
Mobility/stretching		**If outside:** Keep at Z1 to Z2 effort. Work on bike handling skills/ changing gears.	

WEEK 3

MONDAY	TUESDAY	WEDNESDAY
Mobility/stretching	**1450 YARD SWIM**	**43 MIN RUN** (treadmill)

1450 YARD SWIM

200 Z1, rest 20 sec

Use F: 2 x 100 Z1 (25 kick, 25 swim), rest 20 sec btw

100 Z1

Rest 10 sec btw:
4 x 25 Z3
Use B: 50 Z1
4 x 25 Z5
Use B: 50 Z1
Repeat 2 more times

50 Z1

50 min bike

12 min Z1

5 min Z2, build cadence from 70–90+ rpm

5 min Z1

6 x 30 sec single leg drills (alternate legs)

5 min Z2

Repeat 1 more time

12 min Z1

10 MIN RUN (brick)

2 min walk

5 min Z2 run

3 min walk

Mobility/stretching

43 MIN RUN (treadmill)

5 min walk

10 min Z1 run

Rest 20 sec btw:

4 min Z2 at 1% incline

2 min Z2 at 2% incline

1 min Z3 at 4% incline

3 min Z1 (run or walk) at no incline

20 sec rest

Repeat 1 more time

8 min Z1 (run or walk) at 1% incline

Strength

THURSDAY	FRIDAY	SATURDAY	SUNDAY
55 MIN BIKE	**1500 YARD SWIM**	**1:10 BIKE**	**45 MIN RUN**

THURSDAY

55 MIN BIKE

10 min Z1

3 x (20 sec Z2 at 90+ rpm, 1 min Z1 at choice cadence)

2 x (30 sec Z2 at 90+ rpm, 1 min Z1 at choice cadence)

3 x (40 sec Z2 at 90+ rpm, 1 min Z1 at choice cadence)

2 min Z3 at 45-55 rpm

30 sec Z1 at choice cadence

1 min Z1 at 90+ rpm

Repeat 5 more times

10 min Z1

Mobility/stretching

FRIDAY

1500 YARD SWIM

Rest 10-15 sec btw:
200 Z1

Use B: 200 Z1

Use F: 100 Z1
(25 kick, 25 swim)

Use B/A: 8 x 25 Z4

Rest 20 sec btw:

Use S/B: 2 x 150 Z2

Use B: 2 x 100 Z2

Use P: 2 x 50 Z3

Use P: 4 x 25 Z4

100 Z1

Strength

SATURDAY

1:10 BIKE

12 min Z1

10 min build to Z2

7 x (2 min Z2 at 50–65 rpm, 1 min Z3 at 90+ rpm)

3 min Z1

2 x (7 min Z2 build to Z3 at 55-65 rpm, 3 min Z1 at choice cadence)

4 min Z1

If outside: Keep at Z1 to Z2 effort. Work on bike handling skills/ changing gears.

20 MIN RUN (brick)

5 min walk

10 min Z1 run

4 x (20 sec strides w/ 40 sec walk btw)

SUNDAY

45 MIN RUN

5 min walk

5 min Z1 run

1 min walk

5 min Z1 run

1 min walk

3 x (20 sec strides w/ 40 sec walk btw)

3 x (5 min Z2 build to Z3, 60 sec walk)

7 min Z1 run or walk

1600 YARD SWIM

Rest 10–15 sec btw:
300 Z1

Use B: 200 Z1

Use F: 100 Z1 kick

Use S/B: 6 x 100 (1–3 Z2, 4–6 Z3), rest 30 sec btw

6 x 25 Z4, rest 10 sec btw

6 x 25 (odds fast, evens easy), rest 10 sec btw

100 Z1

WEEK 4

MONDAY	TUESDAY	WEDNESDAY
1000 YARD SWIM	**1:06 MIN BIKE**	**50 MIN RUN** (treadmill)
200 Z1 Use S/B/A: 4 x 50, rest 10 sec btw	10 min Z1 6 x (60 sec Z2 at 90+ rpm, 60 sec Z1 at choice cadence) 4 min Z1	3 min walk 6 min Z1 run 1 min walk 4 min run
Rest 10 sec btw: Use B: 6 x 50 Z3 Use P: 4 x 50 Z3	3 x (3 min Z2 at 50-65 rpm, 1 min Z1 at choice cadence)	3 x (6 min Z3 power walk at 12–15% incline, 2 min rest or walk at no incline)
100 Z1	3 x (2 min Z2 at 50-65 rpm, 1 min Z1 at choice cadence)	All at 1% incline: 5 min Z1 run 1 min walk 5 min Z1 run 1 min walk
Strength	3 x (1 min Z2 at 50-65 rpm, 1 min Z1 at choice cadence)	**1500 YARD SWIM**
	6 x 30 sec single leg drills (alternate legs) 10 min Z1	Rest 10 sec btw: 300 Z1 Use F: 6 x 25 kick Use B/A: 5 x 25 Z2 Use P: 4 x 25 Z2 4 x 25 Z2
	Mobility/stretching	Use S/B/A: 4 x 100 Z3, rest 15 sec btw 200 Z2 100 Z1

THURSDAY	FRIDAY	SATURDAY	SUNDAY
50 MIN BIKE	**Strength**	**1:30 BIKE**	**45 MIN RUN**
16 min Z1		2 x (10 min Z1, 3 min Z2 building cadence from 70 to 90+ rpm, 1 min Z1 at choice cadence)	2 x (5 min walk, 4 min Z1 run, 1 min walk)
2 min Z2 (build cadence every 30 sec as 70, 80, 90, 100+ rpm)		2 min Z1	**If outside:** 20 mins Z2-Z3 on rolling hills
2 min Z1 at choice cadence		3 min Z2 at choice cadence	**If inside:** 20 mins Z2-Z3, change incline from zero to 4% every 2 min
Repeat 5 more times		1 min Z2 at 90+ rpm	5 min Z1 run or walk
10 min Z1		5 min Z1 at choice cadence	**1500 YARD SWIM**
If outside: Keep at Z1 to Z2 effort; work on bike handling skills/ changing gears		Repeat 4 more times	Use B: 3 x 200 Z1, rest 20 sec btw
20 MIN RUN (brick or second workout)		15 min Z1	Use S/B, rest 10 sec btw:
3 min walk		**If outside:** Keep at Z1 to Z2 effort; work on bike handling skills/ changing gears	8 x 75 (odds build to Z4, evens Z2)
15 min Z1 run		**20 min run (brick)**	6 x 50 Z1, rest 10 sec btw
2 min walk		3 min walk	**Mobility/stretching**
Mobility/stretching		15 min Z1	
		2 min walk	
		Mobility/stretching	

WEEK 5

MONDAY	TUESDAY	WEDNESDAY
1450 YARD SWIM	**60 MIN BIKE**	**1550 YARD SWIM**
Rest 20 sec btw: 300 Z1 Use B: 200 Z1 Use S/B: 100 Z1	20 min build Z1 to Z2 5 min Z2 at 90–100 rpm 5 min Z3 at 55–65 rpm 5 min at Z2 at 100+ rpm 5 min Z1 at choice cadence 15 min Z2 at 90+ rpm 5 min Z1 at choice cadence	Rest 15–20 sec btw: 200 Z1 Use B: 100 Z1 Use F: 100 Z1 kick Use S/B/A: 4 x 50 Z2 3 x 100 Z2
Use F/S, rest 10-15 sec btw: 4 x 25 Z2 50 Z1 4 x 50 Z2 100 Z1 4 x 75 Z1 100 Z1	**27 MIN RUN (brick or second workout)**	Use F/S: 3 x 200, rest 40 sec btw 50 Z1
	3 min walk 5 min Z1 run 15 min Z2 run 4 x (20 sec strides, 40 sec walk)	**40 MIN RUN**
Mobility/stretching		3 min walk 10 min Z1 run 4 x (4 min Z2, 1 min build to Z4) 2 min Z3 4 x (20 sec strides, 40 sec rest) 1 min walk
	Mobility/stretching	**Strength**

THURSDAY	FRIDAY	SATURDAY	SUNDAY
45 MIN BIKE	**1300 YARD SWIM**	**1:25 BIKE**	**50 MIN RUN**
20 min Z1	Rest 10–20 sec btw:	10 min Z1	3 min walk
4 x (15 sec Z5 at 100+ rpm, 30 sec Z1 at 75–80 rpm)	200 Z1	10 min Z2	10 min Z1 run
	Use S/B: 2 x 100 Z1	5 min Z3 at 85+ rpm	
20 min Z2 at 85+ rpm	Use P: 8 x 25 (odds fast, evens easy)	10 min Z3 at 65–70 rpm	2 x (4 min Z1, 30 sec walk, 3 min Z2, 30 sec walk, 2 min Z3, 30 sec walk, 1 min Z4, 60 sec walk)
2 min Z1 at choice cadence		5 min Z2 at 95+ rpm	
	Use B, rest 10-15 sec btw:	8 min Z3 at 65-70 rpm	
15 MIN RUN (brick)	3 x 50 Z2	5 min Z2 at 95+ rpm	10 min Z1
	1 x 50 Z4	6 min Z3 at 65-70 rpm	2 min walk
3 min walk	2 x 50 Z2	5 min Z2 at 95+ rpm	**1300 YARD SWIM**
5 min Z1 run	2 x 50 Z4	4 min Z3 at 65-70 rpm	
5 min Z2 run	1 x 50 Z2	5 min Z2 at 95+ rpm	Rest 20 sec btw: Use S/B: 400 Z1
2 min walk	3 x 50 Z4	2 min Z3 at 65-70 rpm	Use B: 200 Z1
Mobility/stretching	100 Z1	10 min Z1 at choice cadence	Use S/B/A, rest 10 sec btw: 6 x 25 Z3 200 Z2 Repeat 1 more time
	Strength	**20 MIN RUN (brick)**	
		3 min walk	100 Z1
		5 min Z1 run	**Mobility/stretching**
		2 x (3 min Z3, 30 sec walk)	
		5 min Z1 run or walk	
		Mobility/stretching	

WEEK 6

MONDAY	TUESDAY	WEDNESDAY
Mobility/stretching	**1550 YARD SWIM**	**60 MIN BIKE**
	Rest 10–20 sec btw: 200 Z1 Use B: 200 Z1 Use B/A: 8 x 25 Z3	10 min Z1 6 x (1 min Z2 at 100+ rpm, 1 min Z1 at choice cadence) 3 min Z1
	Rest 20–30 sec btw: Choice swim equipment: 3 x 150 Z2 3 x 150, build from Z2 to Z3 by 150 50 Z1	2 x (6 min Z3, 3 min Z4, 30 sec Z5, 6 min Z1) 4 min Z1 at 80+ rpm
	40 MIN RUN (treadmill)	**1200 YARD SWIM**
	3 min walk 5 min Z1 run	Choice swim workout. Focus on technique.
	3 x (5 min Z3 power walk at 12–15% incline, 1 min rest or walk without incline)	Mobility/stretching
	10 min Z1 run at 1% incline 4 min walk	
	Strength	

THURSDAY	FRIDAY	SATURDAY	SUNDAY
37 MIN BIKE	**1500 YARD SWIM**	**1:30 BIKE**	**30 MIN BIKE**

THURSDAY

37 MIN BIKE

10 min Z1

All Z2, w/ 1 min choice cadence btw:

30 sec at 100+ rpm

45 sec at 100+ rpm

60 sec at 100+ rpm

45 sec at 100+ rpm

30 sec at 100+ rpm

Repeat one more time

10 min Z1

45 MIN RUN (brick or second workout; treadmill)

10 min Z1

1 min build to Z4 at 2% incline

2 min Z1 at 1% incline

3 min Z2 at no incline

2 min Z3 at 2% incline

30 sec Z4 at 4% incline

2 min Z3 at 2% incline

30 sec Z4 at 4% incline

3 min Z1 at no incline

Repeat 1 more time

2 x (4 min Z1 run at no incline, 1 min walk)

Strength

FRIDAY

1500 YARD SWIM

300 Z1

Use S/B/A, Z2, rest 15 sec btw:

150

125

100

75

50

Rest 10-15 sec btw:

2 x 150 (100 Z3, 50 Z4)

12 x 25 (odds fast to easy, evens easy to fast)

100 Z1

Mobility/stretching

SATURDAY

1:30 BIKE

14 min Z1

12 min Z2, increase cadence from 70-100+ rpm every 3 min

3 min Z1

8 x (3 min Z3 at 55-65 rpm, 1 min Z1 at choice cadence)

3 min Z1

6 x (1 min Z3 at 100+ rpm, 1 min Z1 at choice cadence)

14 min Z1

25 MIN RUN (brick)

3 min walk

6 min Z1 run

4 min Z2, 30 sec walk

2 min Z3, 30 sec walk

4 min Z2, 30 sec walk

2 min Z3

2 min Z1 run or 30 sec walk

Mobility/stretching

SUNDAY

30 MIN BIKE

13 min Z1

1 min Z1

30 sec Z2 at 100+ rpm

1 min Z1

30 sec Z3 at 100+ rpm

1 min Z1

30 sec Z4 at 100+ rpm

1 min Z1

30 sec Z5 at 100+ rpm

1 min Z1

30 sec Z2 at 100+ rpm

10 min Z1

45 MIN RUN (brick; outside or treadmill)

2 x (1 min walk, 4 min Z1 run, 30 sec walk)

6 x (4 min Z2, 1 min build to Z4)

3 x (20 sec Z5 at 6-8% incline or small hill, 1 min walk)

Mobility/stretching

WEEK 7

MONDAY	TUESDAY	WEDNESDAY
1650 YARD SWIM	**60 MIN BIKE**	Mobility/stretching
200 Z1	14 min Z1	
Use S/B/A, Z2, rest 15 sec btw:	9 min Z2, increase cadence every 3 min (70, 80, 90, 100+ rpm)	
3 x 100	3 min Z1 at choice cadence	
4 x 75		
4 x 50	2 min Z3 at 100+ rpm	
	2 min Z2 at choice cadence	
Rest 5–10 sec btw:	Repeat 5 more times	
4 x 25 Z5	2 min Z1 at choice cadence	
Use B: 50 Z2	6 x (15 sec Z5 at 100+ rpm, 45 sec Z1 at choice cadence)	
Repeat 3 more times		
50 Z1	6 min Z1	
Strength	**35 MIN RUN** (brick or second workout)	
	10 min Z1	
	20 min Z2	
	5 x (10 sec strides, 50 sec Z1 run or walk)	
	Mobility/stretching	

THURSDAY	FRIDAY	SATURDAY	SUNDAY

THURSDAY

1300 YARD SWIM

Rest 30 sec btw:
300 Z1
Use B: 200 Z1

Rest 15 sec btw:
Use B/P: 5 x 100 build Z2 to Z4
Use P: 200 (50 Z2/ 100 Z3/50 Z4)

100 Z1

40 MIN BIKE

8 min Z1
2 x 90 sec build to Z5 at choice cadence, 30 sec Z1 at 100+ rpm

6 min Z3, build cadence 75–90+ rpm

1 min Z1 at choice cadence

Repeat 2 more times

5 min Z1

15 MIN RUN (brick)

2 min walk
3 min Z1 run

5 min Z2

4 min Z1

1 min walk

Mobility/stretching

FRIDAY

1650 YARD SWIM

All Z1, rest 10–15 sec btw:
200
Use B: 200
Use F: 4 x 50 (kick/ swim by 25)
Use P: 8 x 25 build to Z5 by 25

Rest 15-20 sec btw:
3 x 100 (1 Z2, 2-3 Z3)
6 x 50 (1-2 Z2, 3-6 Z3)
Use F: 6 x 25 (1-2 Z2, 3-6 Z3)

100 Z1

Strength

SATURDAY

1:30 BIKE

15 min Z1
7 min Z2

4 x (45 sec Z2 at 100+ rpm, 45 sec Z1 at choice cadence)

2 min Z1 at choice cadence

3 x (6 min Z2 at choice cadence, 4 min Z2 at 55-65 rpm)

20 min Z2 at 90+ rpm

10 min Z1 at choice cadence

20 MIN RUN (brick)

3 min walk
4 min Z1

4 min Z2, 30 sec walk

3 min Z3, 30 sec walk

1 min Z4, 60 sec walk

2 min Z1 run

1 min walk

Mobility/stretching

SUNDAY

55 MIN RUN

5 min walk
10 min Z1 run

30 min Z2 (walk as needed)

10 min Z1 run or walk

1600 YARD SWIM

Rest 10-15 sec btw:
300 Z1
Use B/A/P: 4 x 75 Z2
Use B: 4 x 50 Z2
Use P: 4 x 25 Z5

Use S/B: 4 x 150 Z2, rest 20 sec btw

100 Z1

Mobility/stretching

WEEK 8

	MONDAY	TUESDAY	WEDNESDAY

MONDAY

1200 YARD SWIM

300 Z1
All Z2, rest 10 sec btw:
Use F: 4 x 25 kick
Use F/S: 4 x 25
Use S/A: 4 x 25
4 x 25

Rest 10 sec btw:
200 Z2
Use B/P: 4 x 25
(odds Z5, evens Z2)
100 Z1
Repeat 1 more time
100 Z1

**30 MIN BIKE
(optional)**

Keep effort at Z1-Z2.

If outside: Work on bike handling skills, grabbing water bottle from cage, cornering, making u-turns, etc.

Mobility/stretching

TUESDAY

42 MIN RUN

2 min walk
6 min Z1 run
3 x (20 sec strides, 40 sec Z1 or walk)
3 x (2 min build to Z4, 4 min Z2, 30 sec walk)
8 min Z1 run
2 min walk

40 MIN BIKE

10 min Z1
6 min Z2, increase cadence from 70-100+ rpm
4 min Z3 at 45-60 rpm
4 min Z2 at choice cadence
1 min Z1 at choice cadence
Repeat 1 more time
6 min Z1

Mobility/stretching

WEDNESDAY

45 MIN BIKE

15 min Z1
4 x (15 sec Z5 at 100+ rpm, 45 sec Z1 choice cadence)
3 min Z1

10 sec Z5 at 100+ rpm
30 sec Z1 at choice cadence
20 sec Z5 at 100+ rpm
30 sec Z1 at choice cadence
30 sec Z5 at 100+ rpm
30 sec Z1 at choice cadence
20 sec Z5 at 100+ rpm
30 sec Z1 at choice cadence
10 sec Z5 at 100+ rpm
5 min Z1 at choice cadence
10 min Z2 at 90+ rpm
5 min Z1

**21 MIN RUN
(brick)**

3 min walk
5 min Z1 run
2 x (5 min Z2 build to Z3, 30 sec walk)
2 min Z1 run or walk

Strength

THURSDAY	FRIDAY	SATURDAY	SUNDAY
Mobility/stretching	**1500 YARD SWIM**	**1200 YARD SWIM**	**45 MIN RUN**

FRIDAY

1500 YARD SWIM

Use B: 200 Z2, rest 30 sec

Use F: 200 Z2 (kick/swim by 25), rest 30 sec

Use A (optional B): 4 x 25 Z3, rest 10 sec btw

Rest 10 sec btw:

Use B: 8 x 50

Use P: 4 x 50 Z3

3 x 100 (1: Z1, 2: Z2, 3: Z3), rest 20 sec btw

100 choice

30 MIN RUN (optional)

5 min walk
10 min Z1 run

10 min Z2 run

5 min Z1 run or walk

Strength

SATURDAY

1200 YARD SWIM

Rest 10–15 sec btw:
200 Z1

Use S/B/A: 300 Z2

Use A: 4 x 25 Z4

500 Z3

100 Z1

1:15 BIKE

10 min Z1

5 min build Z2 to Z3

8 min Z3, build cadence every 2 min (70, 80, 90, 100+ rpm)

3 x (6 min Z3 at choice cadence, 1 min Z3 at choice cadence, 3 min Z2 100+ rpm)

12 min Z2 at 85–90 rpm

8 min Z1

20 MIN RUN (brick)

2 min walk
3 min Z1 run

8 min Z2

5 min Z3

2 min Z1

Mobility/stretching

SUNDAY

45 MIN RUN

2 x (3 min walk, 5 min Z2 run, 30 sec walk)

10 min Z2

5 min Z2

1 min Z4

30 sec walk

5 min Z2

1 min Z4

30 sec walk

5 min Z1 run or walk

30 MIN BIKE (optional)

Keep effort at Z1 to Z2.

If outside: Work on bike handling skills, grabbing water bottle from cage, cornering, making u-turns, etc.

Mobility/stretching

WEEK 9

MONDAY	TUESDAY	WEDNESDAY
45 MIN BIKE	**40 MIN RUN**	**55 MIN BIKE**
10 min Z1 3 x (20 sec Z2 at 100+ rpm, 40 sec Z1 at 75–80 rpm) 3 min Z1 3 x (4 min Z2 at choice cadence, 2 min Z2 at 100+ rpm, 2 min Z1 at choice cadence) 5 min Z1	3 min walk 2 x (4 min Z2, 1 min walk) 20 min Z2 (walk as needed) 5 x (15 sec strides, 45 sec rest) 2 min walk	10 min Z1 12 min Z2, build cadence every 3 min (70, 80, 90, 100+ rpm) 2 x (2 min Z4 at 50-60 rpm, 30 sec Z5 at 100+ rpm, 30 sec Z1 at choice cadence) 4 min Z1 at choice cadence Repeat 1 more time 13 min Z1
1500 YARD SWIM	**Mobility/stretching**	**20 MIN RUN (brick or second workout)**
Rest 10 sec btw: 200 Z1 Use B/A: 3 x 100 Z2 4 x 25 build Z3 to Z5 w/ 10 sec rests 200 Z3, rest 30 sec 4 x 25 Z4, w/ 10 sec rest btw Use B: 100 Z2 200 Z3, rest 30 sec 4 x 25 Z4, w/ 20 sec rest btw Use B: 100 Z2 100 Z1		3 min walk 5 min Z1 run 10 min Z2 run 2 min Z1 run or walk
Mobility/stretching		**Strength**

THURSDAY	FRIDAY	SATURDAY	SUNDAY
20 MIN SWIM (optional)	**1500 YARD SWIM**	**1:20 BIKE**	**1300 YARD SWIM**
Keep effort at Z1 to Z2.	100 Z1, rest 20 sec Use S/B/A: 300 Z1, rest 20 sec 12 x 25 (odds Z5, evens Z2), rest 10 sec btw	16 min Z1 9 min build effort from Z2-Z4, increase cadence from 70-100+ rpm 5 min Z1	Rest 20 sec btw: 300 Z1 Use B: 3 x 100 Z2 4 x 25 build to Z4
Mobility/stretching	200 build Z2 to Z4, rest 30 sec Use B: 3 x 100 Z2, rest 15 sec btw 4 x 50 Z4 w/ sighting 3 x per 25, rest 15 sec btw 100 Z1	4 x (6 min Z3 build cadence from 80–95+ rpm, 4 min Z1 at choice cadence) 15 min Z1	5 x 100 Z4, rest 20 sec btw 100 Z1
	30 MIN RUN (treadmill)	**30 MIN RUN** (brick)	**47 MIN RUN** (brick)
	2 min walk 10 min Z1 run 8 min Z3 power walk at 12–15% incline 8 min Z1 run at 1% incline 2 min walk	2 min walk 6 min Z1 run 2 x (5 min Z2, 30 sec walk) 2 x (2 min Z3, 30 sec walk, 1 min Z4 5 min Z1 run	3 min walk 5 min Z1 run 5 min Z2, 30 sec walk 6 min build to Z3, 30 sec walk 3 min build to Z4, 1 min walk Repeat 1 more time 5 min Z1 run 2 min walk
	Strength	**Mobility/stretching**	**Mobility/stretching**
		OTHER Practice race-day nutrition today.	

WEEK 10

MONDAY	TUESDAY	WEDNESDAY
Mobility/stretching	**30 MIN SWIM (optional)**	**1600 YARD SWIM**
	Choice swim workout. Focus on technique.	Rest 10-20 sec btw: 200 Z1 Use S/B/A: 4 x 100 Z2 Use F: 4 x 25 (kick/swim by 25)
	Mobility/stretching	300 build Z2 to Z3, rest 30 sec
		Use P: 8 x 25 (odds Z4, evens Z2), rest 15 sec btw
		6 x 50 (odds Z4, evens Z2), rest 20 sec btw
		100 Z1
		30 MIN RUN
		2 min walk 6 min Z1 run
		20 min Z2-Z3 on rolling hills (adjust 1–6% incline if on the treadmill)
		2 min Z1 run or walk
		Strength

THURSDAY	FRIDAY	SATURDAY	SUNDAY

45 MIN BIKE

10 min Z1

2 min Z2, increase cadence every 30 sec from 70 to 100+ rpm

3 min Z1 at choice cadence

Repeat 5 more times

5 min Z1

Mobility/stretching

OTHER

Get your bike tuned-up before next weekend.

Write down your gear list for race day.

Fine-tune your race-day nutrition.

Consider scheduling a massage for Mon/Tues next week.

1400 YARD SWIM

Rest 10-15 sec btw:
200 Z1
Use F: 100 Z1 kick
Use A/P (B optional):
8 x 25 Z4

8 x 50 (odds Z4 w/ sighting 3x per lap, evens Z2 w/ sighting 2x per lap), rest 20 sec btw
Use B: 100 Z2

300 build to Z4

2 x 50 Z1

20 MIN RUN

2 min walk
5 min Z1 run

10 min Z2

3 min Z1 run or walk

Strength

1:20 MIN BIKE

15 min Z1
3 x (2 min build Z2 to Z4 at 90+ rpm, 3 min Z1 at 75-85 rpm)
5 min Z1 at choice cadence

5 min Z2
10 min Z3
5 min Z4
10 min Z1
15 min Z1

30 MIN RUN (brick)

2 min walk
5 min Z1 run

5 min Z2
5 min Z3
5 min Z4
6 min Z1 run
2 min walk

Mobility/stretching

OTHER

Practice race-day nutrition today.

Use race-day gear/equipment this weekend.

25 MIN OPEN WATER SWIM (optional)

6 min Z1

10 strokes easy
10 strokes fast,
20 fast/20 easy
30 fast/30 easy
20 fast/20 easy
10 fast/10 easy
10 min Z2
4 min Z1

45 MIN RUN (brick)

3 min walk
10 min Z1 run

10 min Z2
10 min build to Z3
5 min build to Z4
5 min Z2 run
2 min walk

Mobility/stretching

WEEK 11

MONDAY	TUESDAY	WEDNESDAY
2350 YARD SWIM	**65 MIN BIKE**	**1650 YARD SWIM**
300 Z1, rest 30 sec	10 min Z1	All Z1, rest 20–30 sec btw:
Use S/B/A: 300 Z1, rest 30 sec	4 x (30 sec Z4 at 100+ rpm, 30 sec Z1 at 75–85 rpm)	200
Use B: 6 x 50 Z1, rest 15 sec btw	6 min Z1 at choice cadence	Use B: 200
Use A: 8 x 25 Z1, rest 15 sec btw	3 x (6 min build from Z2 to Z4, 3 min Z1)	Use F: 100 (kick/swim by 25)
Use B: 200 Z2, rest 20 sec	8 min Z3-Z4	100
100 Z3 w/ sighting 3x per 25, rest 30 sec	10 min Z1	Rest 10-15 sec btw:
50 Z1	**28 MIN RUN (brick)**	200 Z3
Repeat 2 more times	2 min walk	150 Z3
200 Z1	10 min Z1 run	50 Z4
Mobility/stretching	5 min build to Z4	100 Z3
	30 sec walk	6 x 50 Z4
	5 min Z4	8 x 25 Z5
	30 sec walk	50 Z1
	5 min Z1 run	**Mobility/stretching**
	Strength	

THURSDAY	FRIDAY	SATURDAY	SUNDAY

THURSDAY

35 MIN RUN

2 x (5 min Z1, 30 sec build Z2 to Z4, 2 min Z1, 30 sec walk)
2 min Z1

2 x (4 min Z3-Z4, 2 min Z1)

3 min Z1

30 MIN BIKE (brick, before or after run)

Keep effort at Z1 to Z2.

If outside: Work on bike handling skills, grabbing a water bottle from the cage, cornering, making u-turns, etc.

Strength

FRIDAY

Mobility/stretching

SATURDAY

30 MIN OPEN WATER SWIM (optional)

10 min Z1
3 x (30 strokes fast, 30 strokes easy)
2 min Z2
2 x (5 min Z3-Z4, 1 min Z1)
3 min Z1

60 MIN BIKE (brick)

10 min Z1
6 min build Z2 to Z4
4 min Z1
2 x (10 min Z3-Z4, 5 min Z1)
5 min Z2
5 min Z1 at 80+ rpm

15 MIN RUN (brick)

2 min walk
5 min Z1 run
5 min Z2
3 min Z1 run

Mobility/stretching

OTHER

Practice race-day nutrition.

Use race-day gear/equipment today.

SUNDAY

45 MIN BIKE

Keep effort at Z1 to Z2.

If outside: Work on bike handling skills, grabbing water bottle from cage, cornering, making u-turns, etc.

Mobility/stretching

WEEK 12

MONDAY	TUESDAY	WEDNESDAY
Mobility/stretching (all week)	**1500 YARD SWIM**	**25 MIN RUN**
OTHER	400 Z1	3 min walk
Review course maps.	Use B: 3 x 200 Z2, rest 30 sec btw	7 min Z1 run
Lay out race-day gear/nutrition.	4 x 50, build Z2 to Z4 within each 50 w/ sighting 3x per 25, rest 20 sec btw	10 min Z2
Review athlete guide/event schedule.	8 x 25 Z5, rest 15 sec btw	4 x (10 sec strides w/ 30 sec walk between)
Rehearse transitions.	100 Z1	3 min walk
Visualize yourself succeeding on race day.	**30 MIN BIKE (optional)**	
	Keep effort at Z1-Z2.	
	Recheck any race equipment.	

THURSDAY	FRIDAY	SATURDAY	SUNDAY
1250 YARD SWIM	**30 MIN BIKE (optional)**	**10 MIN OPEN WATER SWIM (optional)**	**SPRINT RACE DAY!**
200 Z1	10 min Z1	3 min Z1	If your race is on Saturday, move each workout back one day to start the week with a swim workout.
Use S/B/A, Z2, rest 15–20 sec btw	10 min Z2	3 x (30 strokes fast, 30 strokes easy)	Don't forget to record your race results (see pg. 188) so you can track your progress!
150	Test out brakes, gears, and check tires for any punctures	2 min Z1	
125	10 min Z1	3 min Z1	
100		**30 MIN BIKE**	
75		10 min Z1	
50		3 x (2 min build Z2 to Z4, 4 min Z1)	
4 x 75, build to Z4 w/ sighting 3x per 25, rest 15 sec btw		2 min Z1	
50 Z1		**10 MIN RUN (brick)**	
6 x 25 (odds fast, evens easy)		2 min walk	
50 Z1		6 x (30 sec fast strides, 30 sec easy running)	
		2 min walk	
		Mobility/stretching	

OLYMPIC DISTANCE

WEEK 1

MONDAY	TUESDAY	WEDNESDAY
2000 YARD SWIM	**35 MIN BIKE**	**2000 YARD SWIM**
400 Z1	15 min Z1	Rest 10–20 sec btw:
Use S/B/A, Z1, rest 10 sec btw:	5 x (30 sec Z2 at 90+ rpm, 90 sec Z1 at choice cadence)	300 Z1
4 x 25		Use F: 200 Z1 kick
3 x 50	10 min Z1	16 x 25 (odds Z4, evens Z1)
2 x 75	**25 MIN RUN (brick or second workout)**	Use S/B/A: 200 Z2, rest 20 sec
3 x 50		2 x 50 Z3, rest 10 sec btw
4 x 25	5 min walk	Repeat 2 more times)
50 Z1	15 min Z1	200 Z1
200 Z2, rest 20 sec	5 min walk	**Strength**
3 x 100 (Z1, Z2, Z3 by 100), rest 15 sec btw	**Mobility/stretching**	
6 x 50 (odds Z4, evens Z2), rest 10 sec btw		
100 Z1		
Strength		

THURSDAY	FRIDAY	SATURDAY	SUNDAY
50 MIN BIKE	**2000 YARD SWIM**	**1200 YARD SWIM**	**40 MIN RUN**
12 min build Z1 to Z2	Rest 20 sec btw:	300 Z1	5 min walk
4 min Z2 at 45–55 rpm	200 Z1	Use B/A:	10 min Z1 run
1 min Z1 at 90+ rpm	Use S/B: 200 Z2	8 x 25 Z4, rest	2 min walk
Repeat 5 more times)	Use F: 200 Z2	10 sec btw	
8 min Z1	(kick/swim by 25),	6 x 100 Z3, rest 20 sec	3 x (5 min Z2 run, 1
	rest 20 sec	btw	min walk)
20 MIN RUN	100 Z1	100 Z1	5 min Z1 run or walk
(brick)	Use B/A/P: 12 x 25,	**70 MIN BIKE**	**Mobility/stretching**
3 min walk	rest 10 sec btw	**(brick)**	
5 min Z2	300 build Z2 to Z3	**If outside:** Work on	
1 min walk	12 x 50 (odds fast,	bike handling skills and	
5 min Z1	evens Z1), rest	changing gears.	
1 min walk	20 sec btw	**If inside:** Keep at Z1-	
3 min Z1	100 Z1	Z2 effort.	
2 min walk	**Strength**	**Mobility/stretching**	
Mobility/stretching			

WEEK 2

	MONDAY	TUESDAY	WEDNESDAY
	2400 YARD SWIM	**40 MIN BIKE**	**2600 YARD SWIM**
	200 Z1	14 min Z1	All Z1, rest 20 sec btw:
	Use S/B/A, rest 10–15 sec btw:	8 x (30 sec Z2 at 90+ rpm, 90 sec Z1 at choice cadence)	200
	2 x 150 Z2	10 min Z1	Use S/B: 200
	2 x 125 Z2		Use B: 150
	2 x 100 Z3	**25 MIN RUN** (brick or second workout)	Use F: 100 kick
	2 x 75 Z3		Use S/B/A: 3 x 200, rest 20 sec btw
	2 x 50 Z3	3 min walk	Use B: 3 x 150, rest 15 sec btw
	Rest 20–30 sec btw:	2 min run Z1	3 x 100 Z3, rest 15 sec btw
	Use B: 200 Z2	15 min Z2 run (walk as needed)	9 x 50 (Z2, Z3, Z4 by 50), rest 15 sec btw
	50 Z1	3 min Z1 run	50 Z1
	Use B: 2 x 150 (75 Z2, 50 Z4)	2 min walk	**Strength**
	50 Z1	**Mobility/stretching**	
	3 x 100 (25 Z2, 75 Z4)		
	50 Z1		
	4 x 25 (odds build to fast, evens easy to fast), rest 10 sec btw		
	100 Z1		
	Strength		

THURSDAY	FRIDAY	SATURDAY	SUNDAY
50 MIN BIKE	**2300 YARD SWIM**	**1000 YARD SWIM**	**45 MIN RUN**
12 min build from Z1 to Z2	300 Z1, rest 30 sec	300 Z1	2 min walk
4 min Z2 at 45–55 rpm	Use B/A/S: 4 x 100, rest 15 sec btw	Use B/A: 8 x 25 Z5, rest 5 sec btw	6 min Z1 run
1 min Z1 at 90+ rpm	100 Z1	3 x 100 Z3, rest 20 sec btw	1 min walk
Repeat 5 more times	Use S/B/P, rest 20 sec btw:	3 x 50 Z3, rest 10 sec btw	6 min Z1 run
8 min Z1	150 Z1	50 Z1	4 x (5 min Z2, 1 min walk)
15 RUN (brick)	100 Z2	**1:15 BIKE (brick)**	6 min Z1
1 min walk	50 Z3	25 min Z1	**Mobility/stretching**
2 min Z1 run	200 Z1	8 x 30 sec single leg drills (alternate legs)	
4 min Z1 run	150 Z2	5 min Z1	
30 sec walk	100 Z3	Repeat 2 more times	
4 min Z2 run	250 Z1	13 min Z2 at 90+ rpm	
30 sec walk	200 Z2	10 min Z1 at choice cadence	
3 min walk	150 Z3	**If outside:** Keep at Z1 to Z2 effort; work on bike handling skills/ changing gears	
Mobility/stretching	w/ 20 sec rests		
	4 x 25 (odds fast, evens Z1), rest 10 sec btw		
	50 Z1		
	Strength		

WEEK 3

MONDAY	TUESDAY	WEDNESDAY
Mobility/stretching	**2200 YARD SWIM**	**50 MIN RUN** (treadmill)

TUESDAY

2200 YARD SWIM

Rest 20 sec btw:

200 Z1

Use F: 2 x 100 Z1
(kick/swim by 25)

Use B: 200 Z1

4 x 50 Z3, rest 10 sec btw

Use B: 100 Z1, rest 10 sec

4 x 25 Z5, rest 5 sec btw

Use B: 100 Z1, rest 30 sec

Repeat 2 more times

100 Z1

48 MIN BIKE

10 min Z1

4 x (1 min Z2 build cadence
from 70–90+ rpm, 30 sec
Z2 at choice cadence)

4 min Z1

5 x 40 sec single leg drills
(alternate legs)

5 min Z2

Repeat 1 more time

12 min Z1

15 min run (brick or second workout)

2 min walk

10 min Z2 run
(walk as needed)

3 min walk

Mobility/Stretching

WEDNESDAY

50 MIN RUN (treadmill)

5 min walk

10 min Z1 run

4 min Z2 at 1% incline

2 min Z2 at 2% incline

1 min Z3 at 4% incline

3 min Z1 (run or walk) at
1% incline

Repeat 2 more times

3 min Z1 at 1% incline

2 min walk at no incline

1600 YARD SWIM

300 Z1, rest 30 sec
Use B: 300 Z1

Use S/B: 6 x 100 (1-3 Z2,
4-6 Z3), rest 30 sec btw

Use P: 6 x 25 Z4,
rest 10 sec btw

6 x 25 (odds fast, evens
Z1), rest 10 sec btw)

100 Z1

Strength

THURSDAY	FRIDAY	SATURDAY	SUNDAY
1:05 MIN BIKE	**2250 YARD SWIM**	**1:25 BIKE**	**42 MIN RUN**

THURSDAY

1:05 MIN BIKE

10 min Z1

3 x (20 sec Z2 at 90+ rpm, 1 min Z1 at choice cadence)

3 x (30 sec Z2 at 90+ rpm, 1 min Z1 at choice cadence)

3 x (40 sec Z2, at 90+ rpm, 1 min Z1 at choice cadence)

4 min Z1 at choice cadence

2 min Z3 at 45–55 rpm

30 sec Z1 at choice cadence

1 min Z1 at 90+ rpm

Repeat 7 more times

10 min Z1

15 MIN RUN (brick)

1 min walk

2 min Z1 run

10 min Z2 (walk as needed)

2 min walk

Mobility/stretching

FRIDAY

2250 YARD SWIM

Rest 10–15 sec btw:

200 Z1

Use B: 200 Z1

Use F: 100 Z1 (25 kick/25 swim)

Use B/A: 8 x 25 Z4

Rest 20 sec btw:

Use S/B: 4 x 150 Z2

Use B: 4 x 100 Z2

Use P: 4 x 50 Z3

Use P: 4 x 25 Z4

250 Z1

Strength

SATURDAY

1:25 BIKE

12 min Z1

10 min build to Z2

7 x (2 min Z2 at 50–65 rpm, 1 min Z3 at 90+ rpm)

3 min Z1

3 x (7 min build Z2 to Z3 at 55–65 rpm, 3 min Z1 at choice cadence)

9 min Z1

If outside: Keep at Z1–Z2 effort. Work on bike handling skills/ changing gears.

22 MIN RUN (brick)

1 min walk

4 min Z1 run

10 min Z2 (walk as needed)

4 x (20 sec strides w/ 40 sec walk btw)

3 min walk

SUNDAY

42 MIN RUN

1 min walk

4 x (4 min Z1 run, 30 sec walk)

4 x (20 sec strides w/ 40 sec walk btw)

3 x (4 min Z2, 2 min build to Z4, 1 min walk)

3 min Z1 run

2 min walk

WEEK 4

MONDAY	TUESDAY	WEDNESDAY
2000 YARD SWIM	**70 MIN BIKE**	**50 MIN RUN (treadmill)**
400 Z1, rest 30 sec Use S/B/A: 12 x 50 (odds Z3, evens Z2), rest 10 sec btw	10 min Z1 6 x (1 min Z2 at 90+ rpm, 1 min Z1 at choice cadence) 4 min Z1	2 min walk 5 min Z1 run 1 min walk 6 min run
8 x 50 Z3, rest 15 sec btw Use P: 8 x 50 Z3, rest 10 sec btw 200 Z1	3 x (3 min Z2 at 50–65 rpm, 1 min Z1 at choice cadence) 3 x (2 min Z2 at 50-65 rpm, 1 min Z1 at choice cadence) 3 x (1 min Z2 at 50-65 rpm, 1 min Z1 at choice cadence) 6 x 30 sec single leg drills (alternate legs) 8 min Z2 at 90+ rpm 6 min Z1 at choice cadence	3 x (6 min Z3 power walk at 12–15% incline, 2 min rest or walk at no incline) 6 min Z2 run at 1% incline 1 min walk 4 min Z1 run at 1% incline 1 min walk
Strength	**Mobility/stretching**	**2200 YARD SWIM**
		Rest 20 sec btw: 300 Z1 Use F: 5 x 25 Z2 kick Use B/A: 5 x 25 Z2 Use P: 5 x 25 Z2
		Use S/B/A: 5 x 200 Z3, rest 15 sec btw 300 Z2 100 Z1

THURSDAY	FRIDAY	SATURDAY	SUNDAY
50 MIN BIKE	**2400 YARD SWIM**	**1:30 BIKE**	**55 MIN RUN**
16 min Z1	300 Z1, rest 20 sec Use B: 300 Z1, rest 20 sec	15 min Z1	5 min walk 3 x (4 min Z1 run, 1 min walk)
2 min Z2 (build cadence every 30 sec as 70, 80, 90, 100+ rpm)	Use A/P (optional B): 8 x 25 Z4, rest 10 sec btw	2 x (3 min Z2 increasing cadence from 70 to 90+ rpm, 1 min Z1 at choice cadence)	**If outside:** 30 min Z2-Z3 on rolling hills
2 min Z1 at choice cadence	All Z2, rest 15–20 sec btw:	2 min Z1	**If inside:** 30 min Z2-Z3, changing incline from 0% to 4% every 4 min
Repeat 5x	200	3 min Z2 at choice cadence	3 min Z1
10 min Z1	2 x 150	1 min Z2 at 90+ rpm	2 min walk
If outside: Keep at Z1-Z2 effort; work on bike handling skills/changing gears	3 x 100	5 min Z1 at choice cadence	**2000 YARD SWIM**
	4 x 75	Repeat 4 more times	Use B: 4 x 200 Z1
20 MIN RUN **(brick or second workout)**	6 x 50	20 min Z1	Use S/B: 12 x 75 (evens Z2, odds build Z2 to Z4,), rest 10 sec btw
1 min walk 2 min Z1 run	200 Z1	**If outside:** Keep at Z1-Z2 effort; work on bike handling skills/changing gears	6 x 50 Z1, rest 10 sec btw
15 min Z2 (walk as needed)	**Strength**	**20 MIN RUN** **(brick)**	**Mobility/stretching**
2 min walk		1 min walk 2 min run Z1	
Mobility/stretching		15 min Z1 (walk as needed)	
		2 min walk	
		Mobility/stretching	

WEEK 5

MONDAY	TUESDAY	WEDNESDAY
2600 YARD SWIM	**60 MIN BIKE**	**2000 YARD SWIM**
200 Z1, rest 20 sec	20 min build Z1 to Z2	Rest 10–20 sec btw:
Use B: 200 Z1, rest 20 sec	5 min Z2 at 90-100 rpm	250 Z1
Use S/B: 100 Z1, rest 20 sec	5 min Z3 at 55-65 rpm	Use B: 200 Z1
Use F: 6 x 50 Z2 (kick/swim by 25), rest 10 sec btw	5 min at Z2 at 100+ rpm	Use F: 100 kick Z1
	5 min Z1 at choice cadence	Use S/B/A: 4 x 50 Z2
Rest 15–20 sec btw:	15 min Z2 at 90+ rpm	3 x 100 Z1
Use F/S: 4 x 50 Z2	5 min Z1 at choice cadence	Use F/S: 3 x 300, rest 40 sec btw
100 Z1	**35 MIN RUN (brick or second workout)**	50 Z1
4 x 75 Z2	2 min walk	**45 MIN RUN**
150 Z1	6 min Z1 run	2 min walk
4 x 100 Z2	20 min Z2 (walk as needed)	11 min Z1 run (walk as needed)
200 Z1	4 x (20 sec strides w/ 40 sec walk between)	5 x (4 min Z2, 1 min build to Z4)
Use B: 300 Z2	2 min Z1 run	2 min Z3
150 Z1	1 min walk	4 x (20 sec strides w/ 40 sec walk btw)
Mobility/stretching	**Mobility/stretching**	1 min walk
		Strength

THURSDAY	FRIDAY	SATURDAY	SUNDAY
45 MIN BIKE	**1800 YARD SWIM**	**1:30 BIKE**	**60 MIN RUN**
20 min Z1	300 Z1, rest 30 sec	10 min Z1	2 min walk
4 x (15 sec Z5 at 100+ rpm, 45 sec Z1 at 75–80 rpm)	Use S/B: 2 x 100 Z1, rest 20 sec btw	15 min Z2	13 min Z1 run (walk as needed)
16 min Z2 at 85+ rpm	Use P: 8 x 25 (odds fast, evens Z1), rest 10 sec btw	5 min Z3 at 85+ rpm	4 min Z2
6 min Z1 at choice cadence		10 min Z3 at 65–70 rpm	30 sec walk
25 MIN RUN (brick)	Use B, rest 10–15 sec btw:	5 min Z2 at 95+ rpm	3 min Z2
	5 x 50 Z2	8 min Z3 at 65–70 rpm	30 sec walk
2 min walk	2 x 50 Z4	5 min Z2 at 95+ rpm	2 min Z3
5 min Z1 run	4 x 50 Z2	6 min Z3 at 65–70 rpm	30 sec walk
15 min Z2 (walk as needed)	3 x 50 Z4	5 min Z2 at 95+ rpm	1 min Z4
2 min Z1 run	2 x 50 Z2	4 min Z3 at 65–70 rpm	60 sec walk
1 min walk	4 x 50 Z4	5 min Z2 at 95+ rpm	Repeat 2 more times
	100 Z1	2 min Z3 at 65–70 rpm	7 min Z1 (walk as needed)
Mobility/stretching	**Strength**	10 min Z1 at choice cadence	1 min walkk
		20 MIN RUN (brick)	**1800 YARD SWIM**
		1 min walk	Rest 20 sec btw:
		2 x (3 min Z1 run, 30 sec walk)	Use S/B: 300 Z1
		4 min Z2	Use B: 200 Z1
		4 min Z3	Use S/B/A, rest 10 sec btw:
		3 min Z1	8 x 25 Z3c
		1 min walk	200 Z2
		Mobility/stretching	Repeat 2 more times
			100 Z1
			Mobility/stretching

WEEK 6

MONDAY	TUESDAY	WEDNESDAY
Mobility/stretching	**2300 YARD SWIM**	**1:10 BIKE**

TUESDAY

2300 YARD SWIM

300 Z1, rest 20 sec

Use B: 200 Z1, rest 20 sec

Use F: 3 x 100 Z1 (kick/swim by 25), rest 20 sec

Use B/A: 8 x 25 Z3, rest 10 sec btw

Choice swim equipment: 3 x 200 Z2, rest 20–30 sec btw

3 x 200 build Z2 to Z3 within each 200, rest 20–30 sec btw

100 Z1

45 MIN RUN (treadmill)

1 min walk

6 min Z1 run

3 x 5 min Z3 power walk at 12–15% incline, 1 min rest or walk (no incline)

18 min Z1 run at 1% incline (walk as needed)

2 min walk

Strength

WEDNESDAY

1:10 BIKE

13 min Z1

6 x (1 min Z2 at 100+ rpm, 1 min Z1 at choice cadence)

4 min Z1

6 min Z3

3 min Z4

30 sec Z5

6 min Z1

10 min Z1 at 80+ rpm

1500 YARD SWIM

Choice swim workout. Focus on technique.

Mobility/stretching

THURSDAY	FRIDAY	SATURDAY	SUNDAY
42 MIN BIKE	**2550 YARD SWIM**	**1:35 BIKE**	**30 MIN BIKE**
15 min Z1	300 Z1, rest 30 sec	15 min Z1	13 min Z1
At Z2 effort:	Use B: 300 Z2, rest 30 sec	12 min Z2, increase cadence every 3 min (70, 80, 90, 100+)	1 min Z1
30 sec at 100+ rpm, 1 min choice cadence	Use S/B/A, rest 15 sec btw:	3 min Z1	30 sec Z2 at 100+ rpm
45 sec at 100+ rpm, 1 min choice cadence	150 Z2		1 min Z1
60 sec at 100+ rpm, 1 min choice cadence	125 Z2	10 x (3 min Z3 at 55–65 rpm, 1 min Z1 at choice cadence)	30 sec Z3 at 100+ rpm
45 sec at 100+ rpm, 1 min choice cadence	100 Z3	3 min Z1	1 min Z1
30 sec at 100+ rpm, 1 min choice cadence	75 Z3	6x (1 min Z3 at 100+ rpm, 1 min Z1 at choice cadence	30 sec Z4 at 100+ rpm
Repeat 1 more time	50 Z4	10 min Z1	1 min Z1
10 min Z1	2 x 150 (100 Z3/50 Z4), rest 15 sec btw		30 sec Z5 at 100+ rpm
45 MIN RUN (brick or second workout; treadmill)	12 x 25 (odds fast to easy, evens easy to fast), rest 10 sec btw	**25 MIN RUN (brick)**	1 min Z1
2 min walk	Repeat 1 more time	2 min walk	30 sec Z2 at 100+ rpm
8 min Z1	Use B: 200 Z1, rest 30 sec	7 min Z1 run	10 min Z1
3 x (30 sec build Z2 to Z4 at 4% incline, 2 min Z1 at 1% incline)	50 Z1	4 min Z2	**56 MIN RUN (brick; outside or treadmill)**
3 min Z2 at no incline	**Mobility/stretching**	30 sec walk	2 min walk
2 min Z3 at 2% incline		2 min Z3	2 x (4 min Z1 run, 30 sec walk)
30 sec Z4 at 4% incline		30 sec walk	8 x (4 min Z2, 1 min build to Z4)
2 min Z3 at 2% incline		4 min Z2	4 x (20 sec Z5 at 6–8% incline or small hill, 1 min walk)
30 sec Z4 at 4% incline		30 sec walk	**Mobility/stretching**
3 min Z1 at no incline		2 min Z3	
Repeat 1 more time		2 min Z1 run	
4 min Z1 at 1% incline		30 sec walk	
1 min walk		**Mobility/stretching**	
Strength			

WEEK 7

MONDAY	TUESDAY	WEDNESDAY
2800 YARD SWIM	**70 MIN BIKE**	**45 MIN RUN**
300 Z1, rest 30 sec	12 min Z1	2 min walk
Use S/B/A rest 15 sec btw:	9 min Z2, increase cadence every 3 min (70, 80, 90, 100+ rpm)	8 min Z2 run
4 x 100 Z2	3 min Z1 at choice cadence	30 min Z2 (walk as needed)
4 x 75 Z2	2 min Z3 at 100+ rpm	5 x (20 sec strides w/ 40 sec walk btw
4 x 50 Z3	2 min Z2 at choice cadence	**Strength**
4 x 25 Z5, rest 5 sec btw	Repeat 7 more times	
Use B: 50 Z2, rest 10 sec	2 min Z1 at choice cadence	
Repeat 7 more times	6 x (15 sec Z5 at 100+ rpm, 45 sec Z1 at choice cadence)	
Use B: 300 Z2	6 min Z1 at choice cadence	
100 Z1	**2800 YARD SWIM**	
Strength	400 Z1, rest 30 sec	
	Use S/B/A: 300 Z1, rest 30 sec	
	4 x 50, rest 20 sec	
	Use F/P: 8 x 25 (odds fast, evens easy), rest 10 sec btw	
	3 x 200 Z3, rest 20 sec btw	
	6 x 100 Z3, rest 10 sec btw	
	6 x 50 Z4, rest 10 sec btw	
	200 Z1	
	Mobility/stretching	

THURSDAY	FRIDAY	SATURDAY	SUNDAY

THURSDAY

1800 YARD SWIM

500 Z1, rest 40 sec

Use B: 2 x 200, rest 20 sec btw

Use F: 200 kick

Use B/P: 5 x 100 build Z2 to Z4, rest 15 sec btw

200 Z1 choice

45 MIN BIKE

8 min Z1

4 x (90 sec build Z2 to Z5 at choice cadence, 30 sec Z1 at 100+ rpm)

6 min Z3, build cadence 75–90+ rpm

1 min Z1 at choice cadence

Repeat 2 more times

6 min Z1

20 MIN RUN (brick)

1 min walk
4 min Z1 run

10 min Z2 (walk as needed)

4 min Z1
1 min walk

Mobility/stretching

FRIDAY

Mobility/stretching

SATURDAY

1:30 BIKE

15 min Z1

7 min Z2

4 x (45 sec Z2 at 100+ rpm, 45 sec Z1 at choice cadence)

2 min Z1 at choice cadence

3 x (6 min Z2 at choice cadence, 4 min Z2 at 55–65 rpm)

20 min Z2 at 90+ rpm

10 min Z1 at choice cadence

25 MIN RUN (brick)

1 min walk

3 min Z1

8 min Z2

30 sec walk

5 min Z3

30 sec walk

2 min Z4

1 min walk

3 min Z1 run

1 min walk

Mobility/stretching

SUNDAY

1:05 RUN

1 min walk

14 min Z1 run (walk as needed)

40 min Z2 (walk as needed)

6 min Z1

4 x (20 sec fast strides w/ 40 sec walk btw)

2200 YARD SWIM

400 Z1, rest 30 sec btw

Use B/A/P: 4 x 75 Z2, rest 15 sec btw

Use B: 4 x 50 Z2, rest 10 sec btw

Use P: 8 x 25 Z5, rest 10 sec btw

Use S/B: 4 x 250 Z2, rest 20 sec btw

100 Z1

Mobility/stretching

WEEK 8

	MONDAY	TUESDAY	WEDNESDAY

3000 YARD SWIM

400 Z1, 30 sec rest
Rest 10 sec btw:
Use F: 4 x 50 Z2 (kick/swim by 25)
Use S/B/A: 4 x 50 Z2
Use B/P: 4 x 50

Use B: 250 Z2, rest 30 sec
Use P: 8 x 25 (odds Z5, evens Z1), rest 10 sec btw
50 Z1
Repeat 2 more times
Use B: 400 Z2, rest 30 sec
100 Z1

30 MIN BIKE (optional)

Keep effort at Z1-Z2.
If outside: Work on bike handling skills, grabbing water bottle from cage, cornering, making u-turns, etc.

Mobility/stretching

50 MIN BIKE

12 min Z1
6 min Z2, increase cadence every 2 min (80, 90, 100+ rpm)
4 min Z1 at choice cadence

2 x (4 min Z3 at 45-60 rpm, 4 min Z2 at choice cadence, 1 min Z1 at choice cadence)

10 min Z1

47 MIN RUN

2 min walk
7 min Z1 run
3 x (20 sec fast strides w/ 40 sec Z1 or walk btw)
2 min build Z2 to Z4
4 min Z2
30 sec walk
Repeat 2 more times
13 min Z1 run (walk as needed)
2 min walk

Mobility/stretching

1:15 BIKE

20 min Z1
4 x (15 sec Z5 at 100+ rpm, 2 min Z1 choice cadence)
3 min Z1

10 sec Z5 at 100+ rpm
30 sec Z1 at choice cadence
20 sec Z5 at 100+ rpm
30 sec Z1 at choice cadence
30 sec Z5 at 100+ rpm
30 sec Z1 at choice cadence
20 sec Z5 at 100+ rpm
30 sec Z1 at choice cadence
10 sec Z5 at 100+ rpm
5 min Z1 at choice cadence
10 min Z2 at 90+ rpm
5 min Z1

21 MIN RUN (brick)

3 min walk
5 min Z1 run
2 x (5 min build Z2 to Z3, 30 sec walk)
2 min Z1 run or walk

Strength

THURSDAY	FRIDAY	SATURDAY	SUNDAY
2600 YARD SWIM	**3000 YARD SWIM**	**1:30 MIN BIKE**	**55 MIN RUN**

THURSDAY

2600 YARD SWIM

400 Z1, rest 30 sec
Use S/B/A: 3 x 100, rest 20 sec btw
Use A: 4 x 25, rest 5 sec btw

Rest 20 sec btw:
Use B/P: 2 x 50 build Z3 to Z5
Use B: 150 Z2
50 Z1
Repeat 3 more times
Use F: 8 x 50 Z3, rest 10 sec btw
Use F/P: 4 x 25 Z5, rest 10 sec btw
100 Z1

Mobility/stretching

FRIDAY

3000 YARD SWIM

400 Z2, 20 sec rest
Use B: 200 Z2, 20 sec rest
Use F: 200 Z2 (kick/swim by 25), 20 sec rest
Use S (optional buoy): 8 x 25 Z3, rest 10 sec btw
Use B: 8 x 100 Z2, rest 10 sec btw
Use P: 4 x 100 Z3, rest 10 sec btw
3 x 200 (1: Z1, 2: Z2, 3: Z3), rest 30 sec btw
200 Z1

30 MIN RUN (optional)

1 min walk
14 min Z1 runn
10 min Z2 run (walk as needed)
4 min Z1
1 min walk

Strength

SATURDAY

1:30 MIN BIKE

20 min Z1
5 min build Z2 to Z3
8 min Z3, increase cadence every 2 min (70, 80, 90, 100+ rpm)
5 min Z1

3 x (6 min Z3 choice cadence, 1 min Z3 choice cadence, 3 min Z2 at 100+ rpm)
12 min Z2 at 85-90 rpm
13 min Z1

30 MIN RUN (brick)

2 min walk
3 min Z1 run
3 x (5 min Z3, 1 min Z4, 1 min walk)
3 min Z1
1 min walk

Mobility/stretching

SUNDAY

55 MIN RUN

3 min walk
2 x (5 min Z2 run, 30 sec walk)
16 min run Z2 (walk as needed)
6 min Z2
1 min Z4
30 sec walk
6 min Z2
1 min Z4
30 sec walk
8 min run
2 min walk

30 MIN BIKE (optional)

Keep effort at Z1-Z2.
If outside: Work on bike handling skills, grabbing water bottle from cage, cornering, making u-turns, etc.

Mobility/stretching

WEEK 9

MONDAY

60 MIN BIKE

10 min Z1

4 x (20 sec Z2 at 100+ rpm, 40 sec Z1 at 75–80 rpm)

3 min Z1

5 x (4 min Z2 at choice cadence, 2 min Z2 at 100+ rpm)

3 min Z1 at choice cadence

10 min Z1

2800 YARD SWIM

300 Z1, rest 30 sec

Use S/B/A: 4 x 100 Z2, rest 10 sec btw

Use B: 200 Z2, rest 30 sec

No toys: 4 x 50 Z3, rest 10 sec btw

300 Z3, rest 30 sec

3 x 100 Z4, rest 20 sec btw

Use B: 200 Z3, rest 30 sec

300 Z3, rest 30 sec

6 x 50 Z4, rest 10 sec btw

Use B: 200 Z1

100 Z1

Mobility/stretching

TUESDAY

3200 YARD SWIM

400 Z1, rest 30 sec

Use S/B/A: 2 x 300 Z2, rest 30 sec

Use S/B: 8 x 50 Z2, rest 10 sec

Use P: 16 x 75 (1–5: Z2, 6–10: Z3, 11–16: Z4), rest 10 sec

Use B: 5 x 100 Z2, rest 10 sec

100 Z1

50 MIN RUN

1 min walk

3 x (5 min Z2, 1 min walk)

25 min Z2 (walk as needed)

5 x (15 sec fast strides w/ 45 sec walk btw)

1 min walk

Mobility/stretching

WEDNESDAY

70 MIN BIKE

12 min Z1

12 min Z2, build cadence every 3 min (70, 80, 90, 100+ rpm)

10 min Z2 at choice cadence

2 x (3 min Z4 at 50–60 rpm, 30 sec Z5 at 100+ rpm, 30 sec Z1 choice cadence)

4 min Z1 at choice cadence

Repeat 1 more time

12 min Z1

25 MIN RUN (brick or second workout)

1 min walk

6 min Z1 run

15 min Z2 (walk as needed)

2 min Z1

1 min walk

Strength

THURSDAY	FRIDAY	SATURDAY	SUNDAY
20 MIN SWIM (optional)	**2700 YARD SWIM**	**1:20 BIKE**	**1550 YARD SWIM**
Choice swim workout. Focus on technique.	200 Z1, rest 20 sec	20 min Z1	300 Z1, rest 30 sec
Mobility/stretching	Use S/B/A: 200 Z1, rest 20 sec	4 min Z2 at 70 rpm	Use B: 3 x 150 Z2, rest 20 sec btw
	12 x 25 (odds Z5, evens Z2), rest 10 sec	4 min Z3 at 90 rpm	4 x 50 (odds Z4, evens Z2), rest 20 sec btw
	300 build Z2 to Z4, rest 30 sec	5 min Z1 at choice cadence	5 x 100 Z4, rest 20 sec btw
	Use B: 4 x 100 Z2, rest 15 sec	4 x (6 min Z3 build cadence from 80–95+ rpm, 4 min Z1 choice cadence)	100 Z1
	3 x 200 (Z2, Z3, Z4 by 200), rest 20 sec	7 min Z1	**55 MIN RUN** (brick)
	Use B: 3 x 100 Z2, rest 10 sec	**30 MIN RUN** (brick)	1 min walk
	6 x 50 Z4 w/ sighting 3x per 25, rest 15 sec btw	2 min walk	8 min Z1 run
	100 Z1	6 min Z1 run	6 min Z2, 30 sec walk
	30 MIN RUN (treadmill)	2 x (5 min Z2, 30 sec walk)	8 min build to Z3, 30 sec walk
	2 min walk	2 x (2 min Z3, 30 sec walk)	3 min build to Z4, 1 min walk
	10 min Z1 run	1 min Z4	Repeat 1 more time
	8 min Z3 power walk at 12–15% incline	5 min Z1	7 min Z1 run
	8 min Z1 run at 1% incline	**Mobility/stretching**	1 min walk
	2 min walk	**OTHER**	**Mobility/stretching**
	Strength	Practice race-day nutrition this weekend.	

WEEK 10

	MONDAY	TUESDAY	WEDNESDAY
	Mobility/stretching	**30 MIN SWIM** (optional)	**2500 YARD SWIM**
		Choice swim workout. Focus on technique.	300 Z1, rest 30 sec
		Mobility/stretching	Use S/B/A: 4 x 150 Z2, rest 20 sec btw
			Use F: 4 x 50 (kick/swim by 25), rest 10 sec btw
			500 build Z2 to Z3, rest 30 sec
			Use P: 8 x 50 (odds Z4, evens Z2), rest 15 sec btw
			6 x 50 (odds Z4, evens Z2), rest 20 sec btw
			200 Z1
			35 MIN RUN
			1 min walk
			7 min Z1 run
			25 min Z2-Z3 on rolling hills (adjust 1–6% incline every 2 min if on the treadmill)
			2 min walk
			Strength

THURSDAY	FRIDAY	SATURDAY	SUNDAY

THURSDAY

50 MIN BIKE

15 min Z1

2 min Z2, increase cadence every 30 sec from 70 to 100 rpm

3 min Z1 at choice cadence

Repeat 5 more times

5 min Z1

Mobility/stretching

OTHER

Get your bike tuned-up before next weekend.

Write down your gear list for race day.

Fine-tune your race-day nutrition.

Consider scheduling a massage for Mon/Tues next week.

FRIDAY

3200 YARD SWIM

All Z1, rest 20 sec btw:
400
Use B: 200
Use F: 200 (kick/swim by 25)
200
Use A/P (optional buoy): 8 x 25 Z4, rest 10 sec btw

8 x 50 (odds Z4 w/ sighting 3x per lap, evens Z2 w/ sighting 2x per lap), rest 20 sec btw
Use B: 300 Z2
Repeat 1 more time
400 build to Z3
4 x 50 Z1, rest 20 sec btw

30 MIN RUN

1 min walk
6 min Z1 run

2 x 10 min Z2 w/ 30 sec walk btw

1 min Z1
1 min walk

Strength

SATURDAY

1:30 BIKE

20 min Z1
4 x (2 min build Z2 to Z4 at 90+ rpm, 3 min Z1 at 75–85 rpm)
5 min Z1 at choice cadence

5 min Z2
10 min Z3
5 min Z4
10 min Z1
15 min Z1

30 MIN RUN (brick)

1 min walk
4 min Z1 run

10 min Z2
5 min Z3
5 min Z4
Walk as needed
3 min Z1 run
2 min walk

Mobility/stretching

OTHER

Practice race-day nutrition.

Use race day gear/ equipment this weekend.

SUNDAY

25 MIN OPEN WATER SWIM (optional)

6 min Z1

10 strokes fast
10 strokes easy
20 fast/20 easy
30 fast/30 easy
20 fast/20 easy
10 fast/10 easy
10 min Z2
4 min Z1

50 MIN RUN (brick)

3 min walk
10 min Z1 run

15 min Z2
10 min build to Z3
5 min build to Z4
Walk as needed
5 min Z2 run
2 min walk

Mobility/stretching

WEEK 11

MONDAY	TUESDAY	WEDNESDAY
1900 YARD SWIM	Mobility/stretching	**2500 YARD SWIM**
200 Z1, rest 30 sec		All Z1, rest 20–30 sec btw:
Use S/B/A: 200 Z1, rest 30 sec		400
Use B: 4 x 50, rest 15 sec btw		Use B: 300
Use A: 4 x 25, rest 10 sec btw		Use F: 300 (kick/swim by 50)
Use B: 200 Z2, rest 20 sec		300
300 Z3 w/ sighting 3 times per 25, rest 30 sec		Rest 10–15 sec btw:
Repeat 1 more time		200 Z3
200 choice		150 Z3
30 MIN BIKE (optional)		50 Z4
Keep effort at Z1-Z2. **If outside:** Work on bike handling skills, grabbing water bottle from cage, cornering, making u-turns, etc.		100 Z3
		6 x 50 Z4
		8 x 25 Z5
		200 Z1
Mobility/stretching		**45 MIN RUN**
		2 min walk
		10 min Z1 run
		3 x (30 sec build Z2 to Z4, 2 min Z1)
		2 min Z1 run
		3 x (4 min Z3-Z4, 2 min Z1)
		5 min Z1
		Strength

THURSDAY	FRIDAY	SATURDAY	SUNDAY

THURSDAY

1:05 BIKE

10 min Z1

4 x (30 sec Z4 at 100+ rpm, 30 sec Z1 at 75–85 min Z1 at choice cadence

3 x (6 min build Z2 to Z4, 3 min Z1)

8 min Z3 to Z4

10 min Z1

25 MIN RUN (brick)

2 min walk

7 min Z1 run

5 min build to Z4

30 sec walk

5 min Z4

30 sec walk

5 min Z1

Strength

FRIDAY

Mobility/stretching

SATURDAY

30 MIN OPEN WATER SWIM (optional)

8 min Z1

3 x (30 strokes fast, 30 strokes easy)

3 x (4 min Z3-Z4, 1 min Z1)

3 min Z1

70 MIN BIKE (brick)

10 min Z1

3 x (30 sec Z5 at 100+ rpm, 1 min Z1 at 75-85 rpm)

3 min Z1

6 min (build Z2 to Z4)

4 min Z1

2 x (10 min Z3-Z4, 5 min Z1)

8 min Z2

5 min Z1 at 80+ rpm

20 MIN RUN (brick)

2 min walk

5 min Z1 run

10 min Z2 (walk as needed)

3 min Z1

Mobility/stretching

OTHER
Practice race-day nutrition.

SUNDAY

45 MIN BIKE

Keep effort at Z1-Z2.

If outside: Work on bike handling skills, grabbing water bottle from cage, cornering, making u-turns, etc.

Mobility/stretching

WEEK 12

MONDAY	TUESDAY	WEDNESDAY
Mobility/stretching (all week)	**1500 YARD SWIM**	**2500 YARD SWIM**
OTHER	400 Z1, rest 20–30 sec	All Z1, rest 20–30 sec btw:
Review course maps.	Use B: 3 x 200 Z2, rest 20–30 sec btw	400
Lay out race-day gear/nutrition.	4 x 50 (build Z2 to Z4 within each 50 w/ sighting 3x per 25), rest 20 sec btw	Use B: 300
Review athlete guide/event schedule.	8 x 25 Z5, rest 15 sec btw	Use F: 300 (kick/swim by 50)
Rehearse transitions.	100 Z1	300
Visualize yourself succeeding on race day.	**30 MIN BIKE (optional)**	Rest as needed btw:
	Keep effort at Z1-Z2. Recheck your race equipment.	200 Z3
		150 Z3
		50 Z4
		100 Z3
		6 x 50 Z4
		8 x 25 Z5
		200 Z1
		45 MIN RUN
		2 min walk
		10 min Z1 run
		3 x (30 sec build Z2 to Z4, 2 min Z1)
		2 min Z1 run
		3 x (4 min Z3-Z4, 2 min Z1)
		5 min Z1
		Strength

THURSDAY	FRIDAY	SATURDAY	SUNDAY
1700 YARD SWIM	**30 MIN BIKE (optional)**	**10 MIN OPEN WATER SWIM (optional)**	**OLYMPIC RACE DAY!**

THURSDAY

1700 YARD SWIM

200 Z1

Use S/B/A, rest
30 sec btw:

150 Z2

125 Z2

100 Z3

75 Z3

50 Z3

4 x 75 (build to Z4
within each 75 w/
sighting 2–3 times per
lap), rest 15 sec btw

50 Z1

6 x 25 (odds Z5,
evens Z2)

Repeat 1 more time

100 Z1

FRIDAY

30 MIN BIKE (optional)

10 min Z1

10 min Z2

Test out brakes, gears,
and check tires for any
punctures

10 min Z1

SATURDAY

10 MIN OPEN WATER SWIM (optional)

3 min Z1

10 strokes fast

10 strokes easy

20 fast/20 easy

30 fast/30 easy

20 fast/20 easy

10 fast/10 easy

3 min Z1

40 MIN BIKE

15 min Z1

3 x (2 min build Z2 to
Z4, 4 min Z1

7 min Z1

10 MIN RUN (brick)

2 min walk

6 x (30 sec fast
strides, 30 sec easy
running)

2 min walk

SUNDAY

OLYMPIC RACE DAY!

If your race is on
Saturday, move each
workout back one day
to start the week with a
swim workout.

Don't forget to record
your race results (see
pg. 188) so you can
track your progress!

ELEVEN

THE FIRST RACE AND BEYOND

//⟶

Congrats on getting one step closer to the starting line! At this point, you've learned about the sport and how to train for it as well as purchased your gear. With a race on the horizon, this is likely the time when you will experience a rollercoaster of emotions—everything from excitement to doubt. To maintain a high level of confidence, avoid a results-based mentality. There's nothing wrong with being ambitious, but your primary goal is to have fun. And if you feel your fitness isn't where you'd like it to be, the race is a celebration of a new lifestyle—one that builds confidence, improves health, and forces you out of your comfort zone. To enjoy the satisfaction that comes with crossing the finish line, a few important details can help you get the most out of your first triathlon event.

TAPERING

Tapering is a gradual reduction in training volume and intensity as a race draws near. It is a necessary component of your training preparation. After months of consistent training alongside a daily endorphin rush, it can be difficult to welcome such a drastic change to your lifestyle. Although your training volume may be less than what you are accustomed to, your body is still hard at work. By gradually reducing your training volume as you edge closer to race day, your body is given time to sharpen up before it's faced with the demands of your triathlon event.

Tapering is often equated with rest. Although a decrease in training load is needed to reduce the physical and psychological stressors that have occurred during several months of training, far too many triathletes are guilty of doing too little training in the week before a race—all in the name of attempting to save energy for race day. To keep your body from getting stiff, stale, and sluggish, you still need intensity and frequency in your race week training schedule. Here are some helpful reminders:

- The length of your taper depends on the event distance and experience. Mini "practice" tapers during training may be helpful to determine the best taper strategy.
- Physiologically, you cannot gain any more fitness in the 7–10 days before your triathlon. It's time to cash out on those training investments.
- With an adjustment to training volume and intensity, continue to maintain a similar workout schedule, but dedicate more time to sleep.
- Be ready for phantom taper pains—weird mental and physical symptoms that seem to only occur during taper. Don't stress if you suddenly feel sick or injured. Trust that this is a sign that your body is healing.
- Don't catch up on previously missed workouts. Avoid the temptation of squeezing in additional key training sessions to give you reassurance that you are race ready. And certainly, don't do anything risky—like rock climbing or playing sand volleyball—during the taper!

PRE-RACE LOGISTICS

There's a lot to do in the 24 hours before the race. Being prepared can make the actual race experience much less stressful. With only one more sleep until race day, here's a helpful to-do list to keep you organized.

❏ Pick up your race packet, which will include a swim cap, timing chip (this may be picked up on race morning instead), race bib, race number stickers (for your bike and helmet), and likely a race T-shirt and other sponsor swag.
Tip: Don't forget your photo ID and USAT membership card.

❏ Review the swim course and make a note of landmarks/buoys to help keep you on course.
Tip: Pay attention to the sun's location to determine how/if it will impact your vision (and goggle lens choice) during the swim.

❏ Walk yourself through the transition area (swim in, bike out, bike in, run out).
Tip: Identify permanent landmarks to quickly locate your transition space (e.g., tree, light post). A brightly colored transition towel/mat will help with this.

❏ Familiarize yourself with the bike and run course.
Tip: Print out course maps from the race website and review in great detail. Make note of any significant sections of the course (steep climb/descent, aid stations, sharp turn, no-pass zone, etc.).

❏ Attend the athlete briefing to learn about any last-minute changes, important rules, cut-off times, and other helpful tips.
Tip: Don't be afraid to ask questions.

❏ Check your bike tires, brakes, and gears before racking your bike.
Tip: Get a complete tune-up on your bike at least one week before the race.

❏ Lay out all your gear, similar to your transition set-up, a few days before the race.
Tip: Pack your bag in order of swim, then bike, and then run gear so that it's easy to organize on race-day morning.

❏ Make your pre-race experience as stress-free as possible.
Tip: Plan your pre-race meals, travel, and logistics far in advance. Always leave more than enough time to get everything done so you don't feel rushed.

Your Race-Day Routine

1. Don't try anything new on race day. Eat the same foods that have worked best before your longest workouts.

2. Give yourself at least 90 minutes before the race to park, get body marked, set up your transition area, go to the bathroom (likely more than once), and do a pre-race warm-up. Pack extra clothes and an extra sports bar and drink in case of a delayed start due to weather.

3. Do a warm-up in order to get your blood flowing, wake up your muscles, increase your heart rate, and get the adrenaline flowing.

4. Don't worry if you didn't sleep well the night before the race. It's the sleep two nights before that really matters.

5. Develop a pre-race routine to help calm your nerves. Develop strategies and rituals to help you feel relaxed and confident.

RACE DAY

It's time to discuss the nitty-gritty details of a triathlon event. Despite feeling physically prepared, lacking actual race experience may leave you a bit nervous and intimidated. Although you may know the ins and outs of competing in a one-sport event, it's not uncommon to experience a bit of anxiety from the unknowns of racing in a three-sport event. From start to finish, the following details will help you plan and prepare for a memorable race-day experience.

Morning

On the morning of the race, there's a lot to do before the start of the event. However, your pre-race jitters may cause you to overthink, doubt your abilities, or make careless mistakes. But know this: You've trained and you're ready—and you have this handy list of steps to follow to keep you focused.

1. **Fuel.** Nerves may zap your appetite at 4 a.m., but your pre-race meal has a few important roles in your upcoming performance. First, it's designed to restock your liver glycogen stores and to stabilize blood sugar levels. Secondly, this meal will keep you from experiencing hunger pangs during your event. Because it takes time to digest and absorb a large meal, it's recommended to eat at least 2 1/2–3 hours before your race start. Race-day morning is not the time to experiment with new types of foods. Hydrate, but don't overdrink. Consume no more than 30 ounces of fluid in the 2–3 hours before the race start.

2. **Check and recheck.** It's finally time to sport that awesome race-day kit! Pump your bike tires, double-check the gear in your transition bag, and do a quick check of the weather. Make sure your bike and run nutrition is prepared before you head to the race venue.

3. **Arrive to the race venue.** After parking, you'll take your gear and bike to the transition area. If you have not picked up your registration packet or chip, this is the time to do so. You will then get body marked by a volunteer. Next, find your assigned spot/rack for your bike and gear inside the transition area.

4. **Transition set up.** Organize your bike and run gear below your bike, set up your nutrition, and mentally rehearse your transition routine. The transition area may feel crowded, so keep your spot as tidy as possible. Make sure your transition area is set up the way you practiced it in training. Take one last glance through the transition area so you know where you will enter and exit for each sport.

5. **Warm up.** To gradually increase your heart rate and prepare your muscles for the demands of the race, skip the energy drink and exercise instead. Start on land (wearing a pair of running shoes that you won't be using during the race) and perform a dynamic warm-up, followed by an easy jog and a few strides with recovery between. Because the transition area closes before the race start, you will want to perform your warm-up in a safe, well-lit area, outside of the transition area.

6. **Continue to warm up.** Change into your swim gear (if applicable) and if a swim warm-up is allowed by the race director, continue your warm-up in the water. Acclimate yourself to the water by slowly entering the water. Then start swimming at a very easy effort for a few minutes. When you feel ready, add in a few

fast strokes with easy swimming between. Your warm-up will also help get the pre-race jitters out of your system. Give yourself time for a last-minute bathroom stop before walking to the swim start area.

7. **Head to the swim start.** Give a thank you to your friends and family who have supported you in this journey and are there to cheer you on. Arrive to the swim start 15–20 minutes before the start of the race. Take note of the swim course layout and water conditions. Before the race, the race director may address any last-minute changes, rules, or details, so make sure to keep your ears and eyes open for any final remarks. As you await for the race start, visualize yourself going through the motions of the race.

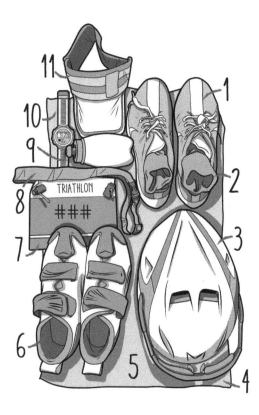

1. Running shoes
2. Socks
3. Helmet
4. Sunglasses
5. Towel
6. Cycling shoes
7. Bib number
8. Race belt
9. Run nutrition
10. Running watch
11. Visor (or hat)

Rules and Etiquette

Most triathlon events are sanctioned, meaning the event must follow specific rules and regulations. For example, USA Triathlon sanctions more than 4,300 events across the country. Because of the nature of the event, triathlon requires a significant amount of officiating to ensure a safe, orderly, and fair racing experience for all participants. It's important that you familiarize yourself with the race rules prior to race day. General rules and common violations include:

- All bike bar ends must be solidly plugged.
- Transition equipment must be placed in the properly designated and individually assigned bike corral.
- No glass containers in the transition area.
- Always follow the prescribed course and stay within all coned lanes.
- Wetsuits are permitted up to and including a water temperature of 78 degrees Fahrenheit. If the water temperature is between 78° and 84°, a wetsuit is allowed but you are ineligible for prizes or awards. Above 84 degrees wetsuits are prohibited.
- You can hold on to a lifeguard's kayak or paddleboard, however you may not make forward progress while holding on to a floating object.
- Your helmet must be on and strapped before mounting your bike. No unbuckling the chin strap until your bike is at your designated bike rack.
- No riding your bike until you reach the mount line. You must get off your bike before the dismount line.
- No drafting while cycling. You must keep at least three bike lengths of space between you and the cyclist in front of you. When you move into the drafting zone, you must make a pass within 15 seconds. Once passed, you must immediately exit the drafting zone before attempting to pass again. In most events, passing must be done only on the left (call out "on your left") before you immediately return to the far right side of the road.
- Cyclists must always obey all applicable traffic laws.
- Never cross the solid yellow line while cycling.
- Your race number must be visible on the bike and helmet.
- No unsportsmanlike conduct.

- No outside assistance from friends or family.
- No littering. All equipment and belongings taken onto the course must always stay with you. You are allowed to get rid of trash at the aid stations.
- Your race number (bib number) must be worn on your front during the run.
- No headphones or music are allowed during the race.
- A timing chip must be worn throughout the entire race. No chip, no time.

Breaking a rule may result in a time penalty of one to four minutes, whereas breaking other rules may result in a disqualification. Additionally, all triathletes must acknowledge and comply with Anti-Doping Rules.

The Race

No matter their experience level, every triathlete goes through a wide range of emotions, from nervous to excited, in the hours before the start of the race. It's completely normal to be anxious, wondering what your body will experience over the next few hours. Although much of the triathlon must be experienced to be understood, it's helpful to understand the motions of the race and how to handle uncomfortable situations calmly.

Swim start: The beginning of every triathlon will begin with the swim. However, swim starts can vary from race to race, with several different types of starting styles. Examples include a time-trial start, wave start, or mass start. For an indoor triathlon, you'll be assigned a time to enter the pool, which is the official start of your race. Regardless of the swim start type, you'll be wearing a timing chip that will record your swim time. When you hear about the chaos of a mass swim start, you may be worried about getting kicked, grabbed, or punched in the first few minutes of the triathlon swim. To avoid the chaos, simply position yourself to the outside or to the back of the mass of swimmers. A time-trial start is much more orderly and calm, as triathletes will enter the water one by one. A wave start (based on age or gender) is invigorating, as you will start in a small group that is less combative compared to a mass start. Remember: Stay relaxed, position yourself based on your swim fitness level (more experienced swimmers will be near the front) and control your breathing before you take your first swim stroke.

Transition 1: Your highest heart rate will occur in Transition 1, as you go from horizontal to vertical. When you exit the water, you may feel dizzy and weak. If you sprint out of the water, you may experience a lower leg or foot cramp. Although you don't want to waste time from swim to bike, give your body a chance to get acquainted to your surroundings. When you are a bit disoriented, the transition area can look remarkably unfamiliar. By practicing transitions in training, knowing the layout of the transition area, staying calm, and keeping your transition area organized and simple, you'll feel more at ease and will find yourself swiftly moving to your bike.

Bike: With the spectators cheering you on, it is easy to push hard right from the first pedal stroke—resist this urge. Before increasing your effort on the bike, give yourself at least 15 minutes to settle into a good rhythm and control your heart rate. Remind yourself that fueling and hydrating on the bike will help your running legs, so don't forget to stick to the sport nutrition plan you practiced in training. You may experience a few low moments during the bike where you feel like you are running out of energy, and wonder how the heck you will be able to run after the bike. Don't let your thoughts get the best of you. Always stay in the moment and be proactive with your actions. In the last 5–10 minutes of the bike, it's time to start preparing your mind and body for the run. Ease up your effort and change your riding position to stretch your legs and back.

Transition 2: With much of the triathlon behind you, you may feel tired and sore. Your mind may even try to convince you to give up. Think about the hard work you have put into preparing for this day. Never stop believing in yourself. Even if the race hasn't gone as planned, stay determined to cross the finish line. Instead of rushing quickly out of the transition area, start with a power walk. When you are ready, begin running. If you need to use the restroom, this would be the best time, as there will be port-o-potties in and around the transition area.

Run: As you make the change from riding to running, your legs may feel heavy and wobbly. The first mile will likely feel the most uncomfortable. Reassure yourself that the feeling will pass by remembering the many brick workouts you accomplished in training. Running too fast out of T2 is easy to do when spectators are cheering for you. Give yourself at least ten minutes to establish good running posture, form, and breathing. During this time, don't be afraid to walk. Remember, there's no shame in walking, especially when it's part of your running strategy. Don't forget to take in fluids and calories. Even if the run distance is short, your body has been exercising for over an hour or two. Continually assess your effort and form so that you can sustain a solid effort to the finish line.

Finish line: All of your pre-race fears, worries, self-doubts, and nerves will be replaced with fatigue, soreness, and pride. As you approach the finish line, savor this moment. High-five the children lining the fencing of the finishing chute and don't forget to smile for a memorable finisher picture. After you cross the finish line, you'll receive a medal for your hard work. Don't forget to thank the volunteers for their help. Although you'll want to finally rest your legs, keep yourself moving. The more mobile you are in the 30 minutes after the race, the better you'll feel the next day. Even if you lack an appetite, try to consume fluids and a little solid food in the 20 minutes after you cross the finish line. Skip the celebratory beer and choose a rehydration beverage like an electrolyte drink or protein drink to kick-start the recovery process.

AFTER THE RACE

Reflecting on a race performance is an important component of athletic development. Unfortunately, many athletes do not remember race information accurately or wait too long to start the reflecting process. Although constructive criticism may prevent small mistakes from happening twice, it's easy to fall into negative thinking patterns— thoughts that are heavy in self-judgment and self-criticism.

Immediately after crossing the finish line, celebrate your achievement. Your athletic endeavor is nothing short of amazing, as you just completed a three-sport event! Give yourself 48 hours to revel in your accomplishment. During this time, assess what went well, strengths, and areas of improvement. Because negative experiences are more vivid than positive experiences, remind yourself that the reflection process should be self-enhancing. Even if a race didn't go as planned, enough went well to get you to the starting line.

Race Reflection Questions

- With great detail, write down your entire race experience (pre-race, swim, bike, run, transitions, finish, post-race).
- What went well? Identify the positive outcomes of your race.
- What needs improvement? Separate your mistakes from things out of your control. If you find yourself too self-critical, be sure to reflect on facts, not thoughts or assumptions.

Remind yourself that reflection is an opportunity to learn about yourself as an athlete, to experience growth, and to help with future training and racing. Although you may feel eager to implement new training strategies to help with your athletic development, be mindful that you don't have to change everything overnight. Stay patient with your progress. Most of all, a productive race reflection should get you excited to participate in another triathlon event.

RACE-DAY CHECKLIST

SWIM

- ❏ Wetsuit (if wetsuit legal)
- ❏ Swim cap
- ❏ Goggles
- ❏ Timing chip (plus safety pin to secure)
- ❏ Swim watch (optional)

RUN

- ❏ Running shoes
- ❏ Socks (optional)
- ❏ Hat/visor
- ❏ Race number and belt
- ❏ Running watch
- ❏ Sport nutrition/hydration belt

BIKE

- ❏ Bike
- ❏ Helmet
- ❏ Cycling shoes/socks (optional)
- ❏ Cycling computer
- ❏ Sunglasses
- ❏ Pump
- ❏ Spare tube(s)
- ❏ CO2 cartridge and adapter
- ❏ Tools
- ❏ Bar-end plugs
- ❏ Water bottles
- ❏ Sports nutrition

OTHER

- ❏ Race outfit
- ❏ Small towel/transition mat
- ❏ Pre-race nutrition
- ❏ Pre-race clothing
- ❏ Photo ID
- ❏ Triathlon membership card
- ❏ Sunscreen
- ❏ Anti-chafing cream, lotion, or spray
- ❏ Post-race clothing
- ❏ Post-race towel

EXTRA

- ❏ _____
- ❏ _____
- ❏ _____

PROGRESS JOURNAL TEMPLATE

Date	Race	Distances S/B/R	Time	Place	Comments
8/17/19	Lake Caesar sprint triathlon	500-yard swim/13-mile bike/2.8-mile run	Swim: 11:17 T1: 2:15 Bike: 44:56 T2: 2:02 Run: 26:22 Total: 1:26.51	12th (30–34 AG)	Choppy swim, wetsuit legal. Hilly bike and flat run. Had a side stich on the run but it went away. Felt really strong on the bike. Perfect weather—cool and cloudy. Had so much fun!!

PROGRESS JOURNAL TEMPLATE

Date	Race	Distances S/B/R	Time	Place	Comments

TRIATHLON LINGO

Acclimatization: An approach or series of physiological changes (or adaptations) that occur in response to heat stress

Aero: Aerodynamics

Age-grouper: Amateur athlete. Age group categories are within 5-year age ranges (ex. 30–34) and gender groups. Race age is determined by age on December 31 of race year.

Athena: Race category for females over 165 pounds

Base training: Low intensity, aerobic training designed to build endurance

Big day: An important day of training, typically of high volume or intensity (or race specific)

Bilateral breathing: Breathing on alternate right/left sides when swimming

Body marking: Your assigned race number is written on your arms and race age is written on your calf with a black marker (or temporary tattoo).

Bonking: Running out of energy, "hitting the wall"

Brick: Combination of two disciplines performed back to back

Clincher tire: A type of bike tire with a separate air tube and tire that sits on top

Clydesdale: Race category for males over 220 pounds

CO2: Carbon dioxide (CO_2) gas, highly pressurized in a small metal container. Combined with an adapter, the CO_2 can quickly inflate a tire when a floor pump is not available (primarily used after changing a flat tire during a bike ride or race when riding outside).

Crankset: A component of the bicycle drivetrain that includes the chainrings and right and left crank arms. It's attached to the bike frame by the bottom bracket.

Dismount line: Indicates where you are to get off your bike before entering the transition area.

DNF: Did not finish

DNS: Did not start

Dolphin dive: Technique for moving through shallow water

DOMS: Delayed onset muscle soreness that occurs 24–48 hours after a hard session

Double day: Two workouts in one day

Drafting: Following closely behind another athlete to save energy/reduce energy cost. Drafting on the bike is not allowed in non-drafting races.

Drag: Some type of object that disturbs the air flowing around it. Can also describe the resistance that water exerts on your body while moving through it.

Expo: Location where vendor tents/tables, race information, and race packet pick-up/ registration can be found

Fartlek: Non-structured intervals that occur within a workout

FTP: Functional threshold power

Hangry: Being irritable and moody due to hunger

LBS: Local bike store/shop

Long course: Half- or full-distance triathlon

Mass start: Swim start format where all participants start at the same time

Mount line: Indicates where you are to get on your bike after exiting the transition area.

Multisport: A sport that includes more than one discipline, such as triathlon, duathlon, aquathlon, aquabike, adventure racing, off-road triathlon, paratriathlon, and winter triathlon

Negative split: Intentionally starting at a slower pace/effort and gradually increasing pace/effort toward the end. When the second half of a race (or workout) is faster than the first.

Overtraining: A decrease in performance, excessive fatigue, or a health decline resulting when the body is no longer able to recover from exercise

OWS: Open water swim

Peaking: Maximizing fitness before a race (typically around taper)

Periodization: When a training season is broken into different periods

PR/PB: Personal record/personal best

Race belt: Belt worn around the waist with race number attached

Race kit: Outfit that you wear on race day

Race wheels: Aerodynamic wheels, often described by wheel rim depth, specifically used on race day

Racks: A designated spot in the transition area to hang/stand bikes

RPE: Ratings of perceived exertion

Short course: Sprint- and Olympic-distance triathlon

Sighting: Lifting your eyes out of the water (typically every 5–8 strokes) to sight a landmark/buoy to help you stay on course

Speed laces: Elastic laces (or shoe locks) for your run shoes. They save time in transition by allowing you to skip tying your shoes.

Split: Time for a specific segment or discipline in a workout or race

Sport nutrition: Engineered products formulated with carbohydrates, electrolytes, vitamins/minerals or other ingredients to enhance performance, delay fatigue and/or to hydrate during exercise

Swimskin: Non-buoyant swim apparel that is worn over the race kit to reduce drag in the water

Taper: Reducing training volume before a race

Time trial: A chance to measure your fitness/performance against the clock. Also known as a swim-start format where one athlete enters the water at a time.

Trainer: A piece of equipment that makes it possible to ride a bike while it remains stationary, typically known as an indoor or turbo trainer

Timing chip: Tracking device attached to an ankle strap worn throughout the entire race, given to you at packet pick-up or on race-day morning

Transition area: Assigned area where you set up your bike and run gear

Transition bag: Bag used to carry race gear to and from the race site

TT bike: A triathlon-specific bike that is equipped with flat handlebars and a set of aerobars

Tubular tire: A bike tire that is glued to the wheel rim and into which the tube is sewn

Warm-up: Preparation before exercising

Watts: A measurement of how hard you work

Wave start: A group that starts together based on gender, age, speed, or bib number

Zones: Effort or intensity to help with pacing/execution

RESOURCES

Active.com: www.active.com
Website with educational articles and events. Often the main source for race registration.

Ironman.com: www.ironman.com
Resource to watch live coverage, read educational materials, and find events within the Ironman triathlon brand

Time to TRI: www.mytimetotri.com
Resource to help athletes and fitness enthusiasts get started in triathlon

TrainingPeaks: www.trainingpeaks.com
Online and mobile platform to plan your training and track your progress

Triathlete Magazine: www.triathlete.com
Triathlon magazine dedicated to helping athletes train smarter, race faster, and recover quicker

Tri Find: www.trifind.com
Find triathlon events in the United States

USA Triathlon: www.teamusa.org/USA-Triathlon
National governing body for triathlon, duathlon, aquathlon, aquabike, winter triathlon, off-road triathlon, and paratriathlon in the United States. Provides resources to empower members of the triathlon community.

USA Triathlon Find a Club:
https://membership.usatriathlon.org/Public/Public/FindAClub
Resource to find a local triathlon club

Women For Tri: www.womenfortri.com
Dedicated to the women of triathlon, to encourage other females to embrace the sport of triathlon

REFERENCES

Dixon, Matt. *Fast-Track Triathlete.* Boulder, Colo. Velo Press, 2017.

Etxebarria, Naroa, Iñigo Mujika, and David Bruce Pyne. "Training and Competition Readiness in Triathlon." *Sports (Basel)* 7, no. 5 (2019). doi:10.3390/sports7050101.

Friel, Joe. *The Triathlete's Training Bible.* 2nd ed. Boulder, Colo. Velo Press, 2004.

Friel, Joe, and Jim Vance. *Triathlon Science: The Ultimate Nexus of Knowledge and Performance.* Champaign, Ill. Human Kinetics, 2013.

Klion, Mark, and Troy Jacobson. *Triathlon Anatomy.* Champaign, Ill. Human Kinetics, 2013.

Maconi, Caryn. "Triathlon: A Current Snapshot of the Sport." *Sports Destination Management.* April 22, 2019. https://www.sportsdestinations.com/sports/individual-sports/triathlon-current-snapshot-sport-16292.

Ryan, Monique. *Sports Nutrition for Endurance Athletes.* 3rd ed. Boulder, Colo. Velo Press, 2012.

Shilton, A.C. "Let's Try a Triathlon." *The New York Times.* Accessed August 20, 2019. https://www.nytimes.com/guides/well/triathlon-training.

Sumbal, Marni. *Essential Sports Nutrition: A Guide to Optimal Performance for Every Active Person.* Emeryville, Calif. Rockridge Press, 2018.

Totaltriathlon.com. "Triathlon History." Accessed July 16, 2019. https://totaltriathlon.com/triathlon-history.

USA Triathlon. "Most Common Rules Violations." Accessed August 29, 2019. https://www.teamusa.org/USA-Triathlon/About/Multisport/Competitive-Rules/Most-Common-Rules-Violations.

INDEX

ACKNOWLEDGMENTS

Writing a book may look like a solo endeavor, but like triathlon, it requires a team. Over the years, I've been incredibly fortunate to learn from many others—individuals who have helped me both athletically and professionally. I wish to acknowledge Matt Dixon, Gerry Rodriquez, Cait Snow, Julie Dibens, and Judy Molnar. With your honest feedback, wisdom, and knowledge, I was able to fill this book with valuable information to help beginner triathletes—just like you have helped me. I'd like to thank the Callisto Media team for its continued belief in me and my writing abilities. I also wish to acknowledge Beginner Triathlete, USAT, Ironman, Triathlete magazine, Iron Girl, and Lava magazine for supporting my ideas and allowing me to share my knowledge. I'm thankful for the help of Dr. G, Chris Johnson, Scott Kaylor, Chris Conner, and Brad McKay for being part of my own athletic journey. I'm appreciative of my parents, Jim (who is no longer with us) and Susie, for constant love, support, and enthusiasm. I'm extremely grateful to the Trimarni coaching team and the many triathletes who I've coached, counseled on nutrition, and mentored since turning my passion into a business. Lastly, I'm grateful to my supportive husband, Karel, who after eleven years of marriage continues to listen to my crazy ideas, supports my passions, and shares my love of all things triathlon, travel, and furry animals. And to Campy, Madison, and Ella, thank you for keeping me company throughout the writing of this book.

ABOUT THE AUTHOR

MARNI SUMBAL, MS, RD, CSSD, LD/N, is a nationally recognized sports dietitian and triathlon coach. She holds a master's degree in exercise physiology and is a board-certified sport dietitian. She is the author of *Essential Sports Nutrition* and *The 365-Day Running Journal.* Through her renowned private practice, Trimarni Coaching and Nutrition, she helps athletes from around the globe prepare physically and nutritionally for athletic events. Her specialty areas include endurance triathlon coaching, body image, fueling the plant-based athlete, and sport nutrition for the endurance athlete. Marni is an elite endurance triathlete who has completed 16 Ironman-distance triathlons (including participating five times in the Ironman World Championship in Kona, Hawaii). She has successfully finished countless long-distance triathlons as well as other swimming, running, and cycling events. She lives in Greenville, South Carolina, with her husband Karel and furry children Campy, Madison, and Ella. For more info, visit www.TriMarniCoach.com.

CPSIA information can be obtained
at www.ICGtesting.com
Printed in the USA
BVHW061907271219
567861BV00001B/1/P